KV-540-794

EDUCATIONAL MANAGEMENT TODAY:
A Concise Dictionary and Guide

David Oldroyd, Danuta Elsner and Cyril Poster

P·C·P

Paul Chapman
Publishing Ltd

QR 371. 203 OLD

Copyright © 1996, David Oldroyd, Danuta Elsner and Cyril Poster

All rights reserved

Paul Chapman Publishing Ltd
144 Liverpool Road
London
N1 1LA

Apart from any fair dealing for the purposes of
research or private study, or criticism or review, as
permitted under the Copyright, Designs, and
Patents Act, 1988, this publication may be
reproduced, stored or transmitted, in any form or
by any means, only with the prior permission in
writing of the publishers, or in the case of
reprographic reproduction, in accordance with the
terms of licences issued by the Copyright Licensing
Agency. Inquiries concerning reproduction outside
those terms should be sent to the publishers at the
abovementioned address.

British Library Cataloguing in Publication Data

Oldroyd, David

    Educational management today : a concise
    dictionary of educational management

    1. Educational planning 2. School management
    and organization
    I. Title II. Elsner, Danuta III. Poster, Cyril
    371.2

ISBN 1 85396 326 7 (Paperback)
ISBN 1 85396 328 3 (Hardback)

Typeset by Dorwyn Ltd, Rowlands Castle
Printed and bound by Athenaeum Press Ltd.,
Gateshead, Tyne & Wear

A B C D E F G H 9 8 7 6

ACC. NO.		FUND
513 151		OAD
LOC	CATEGORY	PRICE
WY	Q R	11·95
2 2 MAY 1996		

CLASS No.
QR 371.203 OLO

OXFORD BROOKES
UNIVERSITY LIBRARY

CONTENTS

INTRODUCTION

ORIGINS AND PURPOSES

This book has grown out of many years' cross-cultural collaboration in the field of educational management. The project finally took shape following the attachment of one of the authors, a Polish educator, to the National Development Centre for Educational Management and Policy from September to December 1991. In the subsequent four years of intensive collaboration on a number of projects much of the material which follows was compiled and the need for a systematic work of reference became obvious.

There is currently a world-wide explosion of interest in educational management. Our target group is this international community of educational managers and management educators. Educators all over the world whose language is not English are reading the literature of educational management, working with colleagues from many countries using English as a *lingua franca* and making study tours or following attachment programmes to English-speaking countries. Each year through the auspices of the British Council and other funding agencies many educators visit Britain to study the ways in which educational institutions are managed. This dictionary is designed to give these second-language speakers easy access to the vocabulary of a rapidly changing field of professional life. It should also be of considerable value to native speakers. Many British educators working and studying in the field of educational management wish to keep up to date with a system which continues to undergo dynamic change, stimulated by a massive programme of government reform and the growing influence of private sector management concepts and vocabulary.

CRITERIA FOR SELECTING ENTRIES

The criteria used for selecting entries to the dictionary were as follows:

- All terms currently needed for understanding what educational managers do; how they are developed; their contexts and organizations.
- Terms from business and general management currently in fashion in educational management discourse and writing.
- Terms now obsolete but likely to be encountered in the literature of the last ten years.

STRUCTURE AND FORM

The book is in three main parts. First, a concise dictionary of terms likely to be encountered by students and visitors interested in the management of education in Britain, principally England and Wales, or readers of educational management literature deriving from the British Isles. American usage is occasionally referred to but no attempt has been made to provide a systematic English–American dictionary. Definitions are arranged alphabetically with indented entries for variants on the key words and are written concisely as single sentences with examples where appropriate. Simple language is employed bearing in mind the needs of the reader for whom English is a second language.

Secondly, a series of one-page long essays which are designed to give a short and simple overview of clusters of concepts relating to common themes. Again, the emphasis is on providing the reader with a concise and accessible overview of selected topics of relevance to the field of educational management. Finally, a list of many of the abbreviations and acronyms favoured by educational organizations and educators. The British liking for reducing concepts, names of institutions and anything else they can think of to acronyms, is highly frustrating to visitors and second language readers, and indeed many non-educators in Britain. Some of the more commonly encountered abbreviations and acronyms are defined in the dictionary, though no attempt has been made to provide an exhaustive compendium of definitions of numerous organizations.

This first edition has been kept deliberately short so that it could be published in the brief form requested by many of the people who evaluated the early drafts. The authors would appreciate suggestions from readers of the present edition for additional entries and other improvements for future editions. These can be submitted via the publishers. At the end of this volume, a bibliography is provided for readers wishing further relevant lexicographic sources.

ACKNOWLEDGEMENTS

Many colleagues and students have contributed to the development of this reference book. Attachment groups from Indonesia, Kenya and Poland stimulated the production of initial lists of troublesome terminology. Special thanks are due to members of ENIRDEM (European Network for Improving Research and Development in Educational Management) from all over Europe, who attended a dictionary workshop at the 1994 Helsinki Conference where they gave feedback on an early draft and offered helpful advice. Particular thanks are due to Eunice Moru, now returned to her job as headteacher in Lesotho, who did pioneering work in identifying troublesome abbreviations and acronyms. Many other British and overseas students of the University of Bristol School of Education at the University of Bristol made suggestions for and helped to assess the accuracy and usefulness of the entries. We also acknowledge the contribution of members of staff of the National Development Centre for Educational Management and Policy at the University of Bristol: Ken Smith and Keith Baker, whose advice on substance was most constructive, and Angela Allen and Norma Meechem who redrafted several versions.

BIOGRAPHICAL NOTES
ON COMPILERS

David Oldroyd is a Senior Research Fellow at the National Development Centre for Educational Management and Policy at the University of Bristol. He has worked on a variety of international educational management projects in Asia and Europe and is currently Special Project Adviser to the European Union TEMPUS-PHARE project in Poland – 'Improving the Administration of Education'. He has written extensively in the field of educational management and staff development and is currently researching aspects of cross-cultural collaboration in this field.

Danuta Elsner Ph.D. is Director of the Katowice Provincial Inservice Education Centre, the largest in Poland. She is a leading expert on educational management in Poland with over ninety articles and three books in the field. Since 1992 she has, with David Oldroyd, co-directed two British government Know How Fund and Polish Ministry of Education projects relating to the development of school directors in Poland. She was Chairperson of the European Network for Improving Research and Development in Educational Management from 1994–5.

Cyril Poster was for many years a headteacher in English comprehensive and community schools until in 1983 he was appointed deputy director of the National Development Centre for School Management Training at Bristol University School of Education. In 1986 he became a freelance education management consultant and part-time editor for the Routledge educational management series.

1

CONCISE DICTIONARY OF
EDUCATIONAL MANAGEMENT

A

academic – a teacher and/or researcher in higher education.

academic board – a group of academic staff in a college or university who advise on academic affairs such as the approval of courses or quality assurance and in some institutions play a role in the administration of examinations.

access course – see course.

accountability – the demand that educational institutions justify to the public the quality of their educational provision and account for how they spend public money.

accreditation – the process whereby one academic institution officially approves the awards of another institution and guarantees that they are of a certain standard, *see validation*.

Act – the final stage of the passage of a law in parliament when a Bill receives Royal Assent and becomes an Act, setting out new legislation.

action learning – an approach to management development where groups of managers from different organizations meet together, often with a facilitator, to discuss the actual problems they face in their daily work before acting to solve them.

action learning set – the group of managers who meet for the purpose of action learning.

action research – a study of social situations and processes in which the researcher intervenes with the intention not only to understand and report, but also to bring about certain improvements.

adaptation – a process of change involving the modification of plans to fit changing circumstances and priorities.

administration – the processes required to support the implementation of policies in organizations, as opposed to the actual formulation of policies which in Britain are more likely to be associated with the term *leadership*.

> **financial administration** – the implementation of all matters concerning budgets and financial accounts.

> **personnel administration** – the process of ensuring the implementation of policies relating to staff for example, appointments, contracts, deployment.

admissions tutor – *see tutor*.

admission system – regulations and procedures for accepting students into higher education.

adoption – an approach to managing change which assumes, probably unwisely, that someone else's innovation can be faithfully reproduced in a different setting.

adult education – largely general interest courses not usually leading to qualifications provided by a variety of institutions for adults, *see continuing, life-long* and *recurrent education*.

advancement – the achievement of promotion.

adviser – a professional, usually a former teacher, permanently employed by a Local Education Authority to provide support and courses for teachers (as distinct from an inspector who evaluates teaching standards).

> **multicultural adviser** – an adviser who specializes in working with pupils from minority ethnic groups and in promoting multicultural education for all pupils.

> **phase/sector adviser** – an adviser specializing in a particular phase or sector of education for example, primary or further education adviser.

> **subject adviser** – an adviser specializing in a particular subject for example, maths adviser.

advisory teacher – *see teacher*

affirmative action – the American term for positive discrimination.

after-school activities – extra curricular activities for pupils which often take the form of clubs, societies and groups including music, drama, debating and sports.

ageism – discrimination on the grounds of age.

age-weighted pupil unit (AWPU) – the factor based on the age and number of enrolled pupils, used in LEA formulae for funding schools.

aggregated school budget – *see budget.*

agreed syllabus – a programme of study in religious education drawn up by local education authorities and church representatives which is not based exclusively on any one religious denomination.

aim – general statements of the direction in which an organization wishes to move; broad outline of purpose.

A-level – the advanced level of the General Certificate of Education awarded after a two year programme of study in years 12 and 13 and usually required for entrance into higher academic education.

allocation – the assigning of an amount of budget to a given purpose.

allowance – a provision of funds for some purpose.

> **capitation allowance** – the sum *per capita* for each student allocated by an LEA to schools, originally for books and equipment, but since 1988 as part of the funding formula in Local Financial Delegation, *see age-weighted pupil unit.*

> **incentive allowance** – allowance on the national pay spine given to teachers who meet one or more criteria, usually connected with additional responsibilities or excellent performance.

> **London allowance** – a supplement to the salaries of teachers who have to cope with the higher cost of living in the London area.

alternative education – schooling provided in an alternative school or by parents in their own homes.

alternative school – *see school.*

ancillary staff – non-teaching staff of a school who assist in its everyday running for example, secretaries, caretakers.

andragogy – the study of how adults learn and the development of methods of teaching adults.

annual maintenance grant (AMG) – the sum given each year to a Grant Maintained School to cover running costs.

appointment – the process of selecting and allocating someone to a new job, usually through open competition in response to job advertisements.

appraisal – the process of collecting evidence systematically on which to judge a person's performance in order to provide feedback, set targets and produce a report.

    appraisal interview – a face-to-face discussion which forms part of the professional assessment process in which evidence is examined to provide feedback about performance, set targets and agree the content of the report.

    headteacher appraisal – *see staff appraisal below.*

    performance appraisal – *see staff appraisal below.*

    staff appraisal – a system of assessing the work of staff in organizations (including in schools, teachers and headteachers) which may or not be connected with promotion and/or pay increases and usually involves systematic observation and a formal interview by the appraiser.

    teacher appraisal – *see staff appraisal above.*

appraisee – a person who is the subject of an appraisal.

appraiser – a person who appraises someone else.

approach – a general direction or method of proceeding.

    bottom-up approach – an approach to strategy whereby the staff in the lower levels of the organization contribute to decision-making.

    top-down approach – an approach to strategy whereby the major decisions are made at the top levels of the organization and transmitted to the bottom.

archetype – a fundamental model or type against which all other types can be analysed for example, leadership archetypes.

articled teacher – *see teacher.*

articles of government – the document outlining the functions of school governors in relation to the headteacher and LEA.

assertiveness training – *see training.*

assembly – a meeting in school time on school premises of more than one class of pupils, sometimes the whole school, usually at the start of the school day, for the purpose of 'a daily act of worship' which is required by law in British schools.

assessment – any means of collecting evidence and using it to judge the performance of individuals or organizations, for example, measuring student learning by examinations and continuous monitoring, or reviewing departmental performance by means of inspection.

assessment centre – a diagnostic testing institution or department which uses tests of competence to identify needs for further training for example, Educational Assessment Centre for Headteachers, Oxford Brookes University; Principals' Assessment Center, Harvard University.

assessment record – the report of the standards reached during an assessment centre diagnosis of competence.

continuous assessment – the repeated assessment of a student's work throughout a course for the purposes both of formative and summative evaluation, sometimes instead of a final examination.

external assessment – assessment carried out by someone from outside the institution being assessed.

internal assessment – assessment conducted within an organization by members of that organization.

assessor – a person who conducts a formal assessment of people or organizations.

Assisted Places Scheme – government grants given to support a limited number of children who pass entrance exams for places in private schools but whose parents cannot afford to pay the school fees.

assumptions – those taken-for-granted beliefs and understandings which underlie argument and action and which often require clarification in an open approach to management.

Attainment Targets – broad areas of learning within subjects specified in the National Curriculum, for example, in English: reading; writing; speaking; listening.

audio-visual aids (AVA) – hardware and software used to enhance teaching with visual images and sound recordings.

audit – a review of performance, usually of an organization, for the purposes of accountability and development.

auditor – a person who conducts an audit.

auditor-moderator – an auditor appointed by an LEA to ensure that standards in the National Curriculum are maintained and to help teachers become more skilful in pupil assessment.

authority – the power possessed by an individual or institution for making decisions and ensuring their implementation.

autonomous – the quality of self-reliance, *see school – autonomous*.

AWPU – *see age-weighted pupil unit.*

B

Bachelor of Education (B.Ed) – a first degree following a four year programme specializing in educational studies and providing practical experience of teaching in schools by means of supervised teaching practice.

Bachelors degree – the first degree after completion of a course, normally of three or four years' duration, in a higher education institution.

banding – the division of year groups in schools into two to four 'bands' or groups of classes based on broad ranges of academic ability.

bargaining – a process of negotiation in which the parties involved give and take resources or commitments in order to reach agreement.

behaviour modification – a therapeutic technique based on behavioural contracts and rewards sometimes used with pupils who are disruptive in school.

bid – an application for special funding such as a research grant or LEA GEST bid.

Bill – the form in which an intended Act of Parliament is presented to the House of Commons, standing committees and House of Lords for its several readings before becoming law.

binary system – the former division of higher education into universities and non-university institutions which ended after the 1992 Further and Higher Education Act upgraded the polytechnics and many colleges of higher education to university status.

bottom-up approach – *see approach.*

brainstorming – a creative problem-solving technique in which members of a team offer many ideas which are written down without discussion or judgement as a first step to finding solutions.

British Council – an organization, established in 1934 with funding from the Foreign and Commonwealth Office, dedicated to promoting wider knowledge of British culture and education and the English language in over eighty countries.

British Standard BS 5750 – a quality standard originally awarded in the commercial sector but increasingly used in colleges of further education and some schools who are assessed against the BS 5750 quality criteria for the provision of services.

budget – a written statement of financial details relating to a plan or institution.

> **aggregated school budget** – that part of the LEA's general schools' budget which the local education authority must delegate to the school.
>
> **general/potential schools' budget** – the whole amount of money derived from national government and local taxes available to a local education authority for financing schools.
>
> **school-based budget** – the budget controlled by the individual school, independently of the local education authority.

budgeting – the process of preparing a budget; allocating resources to specific tasks.

> **incremental budgeting** – rolling budgets forward from year to year with minor modifications.
>
> **zero-base budgeting** – an approach to budget planning which ignores previous, 'historical' budgets and creates a budget based on newly defined needs, aims and objectives.

bureaucracy – a form of administrative organization in which authority is diffused between numerous offices ('bureaux') and a system of rules and regulations ensures, at least in principle, that complex procedures are fairly implemented.

bursar – a post within an educational institution involving financial administration and other administrative duties such as purchasing or the maintenance of the buildings.

C

capitation allowance – *see allowance.*

career – a person's chosen occupation or formal life work.

careerism – the selfish pursuit of personal ambition in one's career by making self-advancement the main priority of one's work, ahead of the needs of clients and colleagues.

caretaker – a person employed to clean and maintain the premises of a school or college.

catchment area – the neighbourhood of a school or college from which most students are drawn.

centralization – the process of shifting power towards the central government, away from schools or local government as in the creation of the National Curriculum.

certification – the process of providing a certificate of qualification to a person or organization.

chair – an abbreviated gender-neutral term for chairman or chairwoman.

　chairman/chairwoman – the role of chairing a meeting.

　chairperson – a gender-neutral term for chairman or chairwoman.

chairing meetings – a process of taking responsibility for implementing the agenda of a meeting by guiding discussion.

Chancellor – the nominal head of a university.

change – the alteration in the state or quality of something, either for the better or the worse.

　change agent –

a) a consultant, usually from outside the organization, who is employed to help the organization to initiate, implement and institutionalize planned change.

b) any person who plays a key role in bringing about planned change in an organization either from within or from outside.

change facilitator – a term increasingly preferred to change 'agent' as it implies helping others to learn how to bring about planned change, rather than persuading or forcing them to modify the way they do things.

change process – the process of initiating, implementing and institutionalizing change by unfreezing of old ways, introducing new behaviours, and the refreezing of new ways of doing things.

change strategy – a broad approach or long-term plan for managing reform.

educational change – innovation or reform within the education system or institutions.

incremental change – change which is gradual and proceeds step-by-step.

organizational change – the planned attempts by management to improve the overall performance of individuals, groups and the organization by altering its structure, policies, procedures, programmes or facilities.

planned change – intentional reform efforts planned and managed in order to bring about improvement, as opposed to the changes which happen in an uncontrolled way.

receptivity to change – an attitude which welcomes the opportunity to implement innovations.

reconciliation to change – the acceptance of reform processes after a period of resistance.

resistance to change – the inevitable tendency of many people to obstruct reform efforts and changes in the status quo.

social change – planned and unplanned modifications in social systems and processes.

Chief Education Officer (CEO) – *see officer.*

chief executive – *see executive.*

Circular – a document circulated by the Department for Education within the education system outlining government policy which does not have the force of law, but offers firm guidance.

civil servants – non-elected national government officials who are responsible to elected politicians and Ministers.

classroom observation – *see lesson observation.*

clinical supervision – *see supervision.*

close-to-the-job training – *see training.*

closure days – days on which the school is closed to pupils so that staff can participate in in-service training, *see staff development days.*

coaching – special tutorial help involving feedback about performance.

code of practice – a set of guidelines drawn up by a professional body to identify the ethical principles and practice to which members of the profession should commit themselves.

co-director – a person who jointly directs an organization or project.

collaboration – the process of working closely together in a way which involves sharing goals and tasks and surrendering autonomy for mutual benefit.

collaborative decision-making – *see decision-making.*

collective decision – *see decision.*

college – a higher education institution which offers awards validated by other bodies; secondary schools, sometimes private.

   city technology college – a school which tends to specialize in technology and science, established in an inner-city area since the 1988 Education Reform Act, with sponsorship from the private sector.

   college of further education (CFE) – a college administered by a Local Education Authority offering courses for those normally between 16 and 19 who wish to take GCSE examinations or more vocational awards.

college of higher education (CHE) – a post-18 institution which provides a variety of academic and professional courses up to degree level, whose degrees are validated by a university or other validating body.

community college – a school which combines the education of day pupils with youth work, adult education and recreational facilities.

corporate college – a self-governing open-access tertiary college.

Open College – an organization established in 1987 to upgrade the skills and qualifications of people in the workplace through distance education.

sixth form college – an institution formerly for 16–19 year olds now incorporated into the corporate college.

technical college – a term formerly used for college of further education.

technology college – a secondary school receiving a special government grant to encourage specialization in technology, *see magnet school.*

tertiary college – a post-16 educational institution, often the result of an amalgamation, which combines the functions of a sixth form with that of a college of further education which was formerly administered by a local education authority.

university college – a constituent college of a federal or collegiate university.

village college – the name given to community colleges in some LEAs.

collegiality – the principle or culture of widespread involvement in decision-making between colleagues which is increasingly found in professional organizations.

contrived collegiality – an imposed culture of collaboration in which colleagues reluctantly 'go through the motions' of collaborative decision-making.

Command Paper – *see White Paper.*

committee – a small official body concerned with policy or management within an organization.

education committee – the group of elected local politicians who comprise the main policy making body on education in a Local Education Authority.

executive committee – a body of people within an organization who are responsible for ensuring that policies are carried out.

steering committee – the body which has final responsibility for guiding the policies and activities of a project or initiative.

Committee of Vice-Chancellors and Principals (CVCP) – the national body at which heads of higher education institutions meet.

communication – exchange of information, ideas or feelings by means of verbal or written language and through body language.

    electronic communication – communication by means of electronic media such as telephone, e-mail, radio transmission.

    elements of communication – sender, receiver, channel (or mode), message and effect.

    face-to-face communication – direct, live communication between people.

    kinesic/non-verbal communication – body language, the way that messages are sent and received through posture, facial expression, tone of voice and other non-verbal means.

    one-way communication – messages transmitted without feedback or response.

    oral/verbal communication – communication by word of mouth.

    two-way communication – active exchange and transmission of messages between two persons or organizations.

    written communication – communication by the written word.

community – a group of people associated together due to common interests either geographically close as in local community (neighbourhood), school community (stakeholders) or geographically dispersed as in community of scholars.

    community council – a body of representatives from the local community responsible for the community education programme and budget within a community school.

    community school – *see school.*

    community tutor/vice-principal – the member of staff of a community school responsible to the principal and the community council for the programme.

competence – having the necessary knowledge and skills to carry out a task to a minimum level of acceptability.

    conscious competence – performing effectively by the use of concentrated thought and effort.

unconscious competence – the stage reached by a skilled performer who is able to carry out a task at a high standard without the need to give it conscious effort.

competences/competencies – specific skills or elements of performance.

competency-based evaluation/standards – assessment based on the observation of the performance of specific tasks in relation to a specified minimum level of acceptability.

competitive tendering – the legal requirement of local education authorities or educational institutions to seek several estimates of costs (tenders) from different suppliers before goods or services are purchased.

comprehensive education – the provision of non-selective schools, introduced gradually in England and Wales from the 1960s, *see school.*

compulsory competitive tendering – *see competitive tendering.*

conditions of service – the requirements of an employee by an employer often set out in a contract, or in the case of teachers, in an Education Act.

conference – a large organized gathering of people who meet for the purpose of professional learning or to hear important presentations from leading figures in their fields.

conflict – a situation where contradictory interests come face to face.

  conflict management/resolution – the process of finding a solution to a clash of contradictory interests.

consensus – an agreement to which all involved are committed without necessarily putting the matter to a vote.

consortium –

a) a group or federation of educational institutions who collaborate for mutual benefit, for example, in offering complementary courses and timetables in order to broaden student choice.

b) a regional grouping of LEAs who work together on a major initiative such as TVEI.

consultant – an expert, often self-employed or working for a private firm, who provides professional support and strategic advice to organizations and institutions about structures, processes and tasks.

  educational management consultant – specialist in providing process or task advice and support to school and local authority leaders.

image consultant – a specialist from the field of commercial marketing increasingly used by schools driven by market forces to try to improve their image in the community 'market place'.

OD consultant – *see organizational development.*

process consultant – one who provides advice about organizational design, functioning and improvement.

task consultant – one who provides expert support in solving specific technical problems or implementing specific innovations.

consultation – seeking or providing advice in order to improve the quality of decisions.

contact ratio – the proportion of the week in which, in a given school, teachers are engaged in direct teaching.

contact time – the time spent each week by a lecturer or teacher in formal face-to-face teaching or tutoring with students.

context – the situation which surrounds an event, institution or process and which may define needs or influence performance.

contingency theory – the assumption that leadership style needs to be modified in relation to the situation or the level of experience of the followers, *see leadership – situational leadership.*

continuing education – the notion that education, both formal and informal, should last throughout life, beyond the level of compulsory schooling and the acquisition of initial qualifications.

continuous assessment – *see assessment.*

contract – an agreement, usually written, between two or more parties, normally enforceable by law.

contract researcher – a researcher employed for a fixed period only and who is not a permanent member of staff of the institution concerned.

employment contract – the agreement between employer and employee outlining the obligations of both parties in relation to conditions of service, remuneration, pensions.

permanent contract – an agreement in which an employee is appointed as a permanent member of staff, presumably until retirement.

research contract – the agreement between a funding body and an institution receiving a research grant.

short-term contract – a contract of short duration, typically one term or one year in the case of teachers, lecturers or researchers.

control/controlling – the process of exercising influence or power over people, purposes, processes or outcomes.

co-operation – a process in which different individuals, groups or organizations pursue similar purposes harmoniously without a major surrender of autonomy.

co-ordination – the act of making sure that separate processes or events are implemented harmoniously.

co-ordinator – the person responsible for making sure that separate processes are implemented harmoniously.

> **curriculum co-ordinator** – *see curriculum.*
>
> **LEA co-ordinator** – a person who co-ordinates a project across a whole local education authority.
>
> **regional co-ordinator** – a co-ordinator of projects involving several local education authorities.
>
> **TVEI co-ordinator** – the person appointed to manage the implementation of the Technical and Vocational Education Initiative at regional, local educational or school levels.

core subjects – *see subject.*

council – an official assembly or organization of councillors, representatives or appointees as in an elected local County Council, a student council or a national body such as the Higher Education Funding Council for England.

Council for National Academic Awards (CNAA) – a national body which validates courses and degrees from higher education institutes which themselves, unlike universities, are not self-validating.

councillor – an official member of a council.

counselling – verbal help given by a trained counsellor to clients such as pupils, teachers or headteachers in order to clarify needs, motives and reasons for action by encouraging the client to reach his/her own conclusions about appropriate action, relationships and resources.

counsellor – a person who provides counselling.

counterpart – a term sometimes used to describe colleagues from different countries who share similar responsibilities in an international project, for example, co-directors or special advisers.

course – an extended learning experience around a general subject or theme provided as part of formal education.

> **access course** – a course run by a higher education institution or approved college for students lacking 'standard entrance qualifications' who want to get access to other courses.

coursework – the body of assessed assignments submitted by a student which, along with or instead of a final examination, determine success or failure.

degree course – a course leading to the award of a degree.

foundation course – a general introductory course which lays a foundation for more specialist courses.

in-service course – a course for practising professionals who are already qualified as a result of initial training.

link course – a course run jointly by two educational institutions, for example, a school and a college of further education.

long course – a planned learning experience extending over several weeks or years, usually leading to qualifications.

pre-service course – a course which prepares professionals for their careers, leading to basic entry qualifications, *see Bachelor of Education, Post-graduate Certificate in Education.*

refresher course – a course provided to update a qualified person.

sandwich course – a vocational course in which studies in college alternate with periods of work in the job for which the student is being educated.

short course – a planned learning experience lasting up to a week or 30 hours, often not leading to qualifications.

Credit Accumulation and Transfer Scheme (CATS) – a national framework for transferring academic credits between higher education institutions.

credits/credit points – numerical values attached to completed study units or modules which can be accumulated towards a qualification, *see module.*

credit transfer – a scheme which allows the transfer between higher educational institutions of credits earned for the successful completion of study units.

criterion (pl. criteria) – a characteristic or standard on which a judgement or evaluation can be based.

criterion-referenced test – *see test.*

critical friend – the term used for a colleague who is trusted to provide open and honest feedback about professional performance, for example in coaching or mutual observation.

cross-curricular elements – the content within the National Curriculum which has to be incorporated into the teaching of several core and foundation subjects for example, 'dimensions' such as equal opportunities or 'themes' such as economic and industrial understanding, health education, environmental education.

culture – *see organizational culture.*

cultural minority – *see group.*

curriculum –

a) a 'programme for instruction' designed in an educational institution.

b) all the learning that takes place in a school or other institution, both planned and unplanned.

    basic curriculum – the curriculum which all pupils must receive in schools between ages 5 and 16, including core and foundation subjects plus religious education.

    common curriculum – a curriculum planned to cater for all pupils in a school which is 'common' in the sense that all pupils study certain subjects or have certain educational experiences by the time they leave school.

    compulsory curriculum – that part of either a national or school's curriculum which all pupils must study.

    core curriculum – that part of the curriculum which is considered sufficiently important to be made compulsory for all students.

    curriculum co-ordinator – a post of responsibility for co-ordinating the work of teachers relating to short-term curriculum projects, for example, Technical and Vocational Education Initiative or cross-curricular themes, for example, environmental education or information technology.

    curriculum development – the process of improving the formal learning activities carried out in schools by providing new courses or learning resources, improving existing programmes and methods of teaching and assessment.

    curriculum guidelines – notes provided for teachers to help them organize and teach a particular subject in the curriculum.

    curriculum panel/working party – a group of staff given the responsibility of reviewing and advising on curricula across a whole institution.

    curriculum review – a systematic evaluation of the formal learning courses and activities provided by an educational system, institution or department in order to identify areas for improvement.

    hidden curriculum – the attitudes and behaviour patterns learned by pupils from their experience of schooling which are not intended by school authorities.

National Curriculum – the legally required framework of core and foundation subjects which must be taught by all (except private) schools in England and Wales to children between the ages of 5 and 16 (Key Stages 1 to 4).

optional curriculum – that part of a curriculum which can be chosen but which is not compulsory.

D

data (pl.) – basic items of information either numerical or linguistic.

> **data bank** – a place where information is stored so that it can be retrieved or accessed.

> **database** – a place where information is stored on a computer, as on a spreadsheet.

> **'hard' data** – measurable, low-inference data which can be quantified objectively.

> **'soft' data** – speculative, high-inference data which cannot be measured precisely.

datum – the singular noun of 'data' meaning an individual item of information.

Dean – the person responsible for a faculty or group of departments in a university or a higher education institution.

decentralization – the shifting of power away from national or central authorities towards regional or local authorities, or from local authorities to individual institutions as in the delegation of financing to schools under Local Financial Management.

decision – the point at which a commitment to a course of action is agreed.

> **collective decision** – a decision made jointly, resulting in a sense of ownership by all parties of what is decided.

> **executive decision** – a decision made by the top management or chief executive of an organization.

> **unilateral decision** – a decision made without taking into account the wishes of other interested parties.

decision-making – the steps through which one goes in arriving at a decision.

> **collaborative decision-making** – decisions arrived at through a

process of mutual sharing and open contribution from all concerned.

consultative decision-making – a process whereby leaders consult followers before taking key decisions which they will have to implement.

decode a message – *see message.*

degree – a qualification awarded by universities and other institutions of higher education on successful completion of a degree course at one of three levels: bachelor, master and doctor.

class of degree – grades – first, second (upper and lower) or third class – into which an honours degree is classified.

external degree – a degree awarded by a higher education institution to students who do not attend that university, but study elsewhere.

first degree – the initial higher education award at degree, usually bachelors level.

higher degree – a postgraduate degree beyond the level of a first or bachelors' degree.

honorary degree – a degree awarded as an honour for distinguished people who have not followed a programme of study for that degree.

honours degree – a specialist degree with a greater emphasis on one subject than in a general degree.

delayering – the removal of layers of middle management in a hierarchic structure in order to produce a flatter organizational structure.

delegatee – a person to whom authority is delegated.

delegation –
a) the process by which authority, budgets and tasks are distributed downwards in a system or organization.
b) a group which visits a country or organization in order to act as special representatives or to present a special case or grievance.

delegator – a person who delegates authority to others.

delinquent pupil – *see pupil.*

department –
a) an administrative sub-division of an organization;
b) a sub-division of a faculty or a team within an educational institution responsible for a specific part of the curriculum, for example, Geography Department.

Department for Education (DFE) – *see Ministry of Education.*

Deputy Chief Education Officer – *see officer.*

deputy head – the second most senior rank within the hierarchy of a school.

deschooling – a movement which emerged in the 1960s which made a critique of conventional schooling and advocated community-based alternatives, particularly in relation to developing countries where schools were seen as raising expectations which could never be fulfilled.

development – the act or process of growing or improving.

   academic development – a term used for curriculum development in higher education.

   curriculum development – *see curriculum.*

   human resource development (HRD) – the process of improving the capacity of the people in an organization to achieve its goals.

   management development (MD) – leadership education and training for middle or top-level personnel to upgrade their skills and knowledge; improving the structures, processes and culture within an organization in order better to achieve organizational goals.

   management self-development (MSD) – the engagement of a manager, mainly alone, in development activities which improve understanding and performance of the tasks of management.

   organizational development (OD) – a process of consultancy and training to modify organizational structures, roles, processes and culture in order to adapt to demands placed on the institution by the environment.

   professional development – the process of developing the capacities, skills and understandings of a person in a professional occupation.

   staff development – a process and activities designed to improve staff and organizational knowledge, skills and performance.

development activities – planned learning experiences designed to promote improvement of practice.

didactics – the technical term, little used in Britain, for the science of pedagogy.

didactic teaching – teaching with a heavy emphasis on formal expository instruction.

differentiation – the matching of pupils' work to the differing capabilities of individuals or groups.

diploma – a pre- or post-degree qualification granted by an institution at the end of a course of study.

Diploma of Higher Education (Dip.HE) – an award obtained after a two-year course of study at undergraduate level.

directed time – that part of the working year in which teachers have a statutory obligation to carry out duties specified in their job descriptions for example, 1265 hours per year specified in the 1986 Education Act.

director – the most senior position in certain organizations.

    Director of Education – another term for Chief Education Officer, *see officer*.

    Director of Studies/Academic Development – the title of a senior member of staff in a school or higher education institution who has overall responsibility for managing the curriculum.

    managing director – the director of a company, usually in the private sector for example, educational management consultancy or publishing firm.

disaggregation – the splitting up of administrative areas such as counties into smaller unitary districts or local authorities.

disapplication – the process of removing the obligation of a pupil to be taught all subjects of the National Curriculum where this would not be appropriate due to special learning difficulties.

disbursements – payments made from a budget.

discretionary award – a grant to students awarded by an LEA based on individual assessment of eligibility using the LEA's own criteria, *see mandatory award*.

disruptive unit – a special, heavily staffed unit within a school or LEA to which pupils with severe behavioural difficulties are sent, either part-time or full-time.

dissemination – the process of making available the results of research and development or information about good practice through a variety of strategies such as publication, conferences or networks.

dissertation – a lengthy report of research or scholarship which is submitted in order to gain a higher degree, usually at masters' or doctoral levels, *see thesis*.

distance learning – a formal study programme where the teacher is distanced from the learner who uses pre-produced materials, video tapes and other media for self-instruction, usually supplemented by some tutorial support.

distance action learning – a type of self-development promoted by a distance learning programme which involves self-diagnosis and problem-solving action with colleagues.

distance learning materials – print or multimedia learning materials designed to support distance learning.

Doctor of Education (Ed.D.) – an award based on a combined programme of taught courses and research dissertation.

Doctor of Philosophy (Ph.D.) – an award based on a major research project, usually of three years' duration.

Doctors degree/Doctorate – the highest academic award usually awarded as a result of research, in the form of a thesis.

don – a term formerly used to describe fellows of Oxford and Cambridge universities but now used to describe university lecturers in general.

down-sizing – the process of reducing the size of an organization and its workforce.

driving forces – *see force-field analysis.*

dyad – a pair of people who work together in a training workshop activity.

dynamic – the qualities of high energy and a constant search for action and change which characterize some leaders and organizations.

E

EBD pupil – *see pupil.*

education –

a) the intentional process of providing learners with systematic opportunities to acquire knowledge, skills and values through a variety of learning activities, usually involving teaching.

b) the multidisciplinary field of study encompassing teaching and learning, andragogy, didactics, pedagogy and related social science disciplines.

Education Act – laws passed by parliament to regulate the education system, for example, 1988 Education Reform Act, 1992 Further and Higher Education Act.

educational change – *see change.*

educational management consultant – *see consultant.*

educational provision – all resources and services provided for the purposes of education.

Educational Psychology Service – the team of educational psychologists either within a local education authority or, increasingly, privatized which serves pupils in need of psychological diagnosis and support.

Educational Welfare Service (EWS) – the local authority organization of educational welfare officers who enforce compulsory school attendance and provide welfare support such as clothing grants or free school meal grants to pupils in need, *see officer.*

Education Association (EA) – a small task force appointed by the Secretary of State to take over from governors and senior management team the management of a school judged by inspectors 'at risk' of failing to give pupils a suitable education.

education committee – the group of locally elected politicians in a county council or district who take responsibility for Local Education Authority policy making and to whom local officials are accountable.

education establishment – a somewhat derogatory and vague term referring to those senior professionals in the education system who are seen by certain politicians as wielding too much influence over the system as a whole.

education officer – *see officer.*

Education Otherwise – an organization for parents who exercise their legal right to educate their children at home.

Education Reform Act – the largest single Education Act for many decades which was passed in 1988 and which consolidated the Conservative government's policy of introducing a centralized National Curriculum, decentralizing financial management and reducing the powers of LEAs and using market forces in the education system.

education voucher system – a proposed scheme whereby vouchers would be given to parents to enable them to purchase education at schools of their choice.

effectiveness – the extent to which goals or purposes are achieved.

effective school – *see school.*

effective schools movement – the community of researchers which has attempted to measure the extent to which schools enhance pupil learning and the factors which contribute to this process.

efficacy – the degree of mastery or sense of effectiveness felt by an individual, group or organization.

efficiency – the extent to which results are achieved with the minimum effort and resource.

elements of communication – *see communication.*

eleven plus examination – tests administered to eleven year old pupils by LEAs in which selective grammar schools still accept only pupils able to pass such a test.

emeritus – a title given to a distinguished professor or a reader as an honour on his or her retirement.

employee – someone who is contracted to or works for an employer.

employer – a person who contractually employs or provides work for an employee.

employment – the state of having a job, usually a paid and contracted job.

>**full-time employment** – employment for a full working week.

>**part-time employment** – employment for less than a full working week.

>**underemployment** – the failure to use fully an employee's available time and skills.

empowerment – giving responsibility and a share in decision-making to subordinates in order to encourage 'ownership' of policy, shared leadership and high levels of performance.

encode a message – *see message.*

end of key stage descriptions – the statements in the National Curriculum which set out the standard of performance expected of the majority of pupils at the end of each key stage.

enrolment – a list of people who join or belong to an institution, course or class.

>**open enrolment** – the freedom of parents to enrol their children at a school of their choice which is the way in which, since the 1988 Education Reform Act, market forces have been incorporated into the education system encouraging schools to compete for pupils.

entrepreneur – a person who assumes the risk of a business venture.

entrepreneurialism – the introduction into the public services such as education of opportunities for generating income by means of risk-taking enterprises in the same way as in business organizations.

entry qualification – the formal academic requirements needed to gain entry to a higher education course.

environment – surroundings or situation as in classroom environment, school environment, including physical, aesthetic, social and other variables.

equal opportunities – a trend towards the elimination of discrimination on the grounds of gender or marital status, race, disability, sexual orientation, age, ethnic origin.

equilibrium – a state of stability or balance of forces.

ethnic minority – *see group.*

evaluation – judging the worth or value of something, for example, a situation, process, product, result.

> **evaluation criteria** – the qualities or desired characteristics against which the subjects of evaluation are judged.
>
> **formative evaluation** – making judgements about a process or project while it is in progress, in order to improve.
>
> **ipsative evaluation** – making a judgement about present performance against past performance.
>
> **qualitative evaluation** – based on subjective judgement using 'soft' data.
>
> **quantitative evaluation** – based on objective measurement using 'hard' data.
>
> **summative evaluation** – making a final judgement at the completion of a process or project to sum up results.

examinations board – one of the five bodies which administer the GCSE and A-level examinations taken by students in schools in England and Wales.

exceptional performance – the term used to describe an unusually high level of attainment in the National Curriculum beyond the highest numbered level – level eight.

exclusion – the temporary or permanent banning of a student from school because of serious behaviour problems, subject to appeal by parents to the governing body and the LEA.

executive – a top administrator or manager in a business or public organization, for example, Chief Executive of a County Council.

> **chief executive** – the most senior administrator of an organization to whom all other administrators are responsible.
>
> **executive briefing** – a meeting to provide a group of executives such as headteachers with information on a matter of current interest or importance.
>
> **executive committee** – *see committee.*
>
> **executive decision** – *see decision.*

experiential learning/training – learning by doing or through direct practice as opposed to theory.

external degree – *see degree.*

external examiner – an academic from one university or college who, as part of a quality assurance process, examines each year a cross-section of students' assignments, examination scripts and dissertations to ensure that they are marked to an appropriate standard.

extra-curricular activities – *see after-school activities.*

extra-mural education – the courses offered to the general public by university departments of continuing or adult education.

F

facilitate – to help or to make it possible for something to be achieved.

facilitator – a person who assists others to achieve success.

facilities – the physical materials and buildings provided by an institution to make it possible to carry out its functions.

faculty –

a) an administrative unit responsible for a specific part of the curriculum within a school or higher education institution usually consisting of a group of departments.

b) an American term meaning all the teaching staff of a school or university.

    Faculty of Education – that unit within a university which provides courses for pre-service and in-service teachers and educational managers and in which educational research is conducted.

feasibility study – a preliminary study which is often undertaken before launching a research or development project in order to assess the possibility of success.

feedback – providing information to learners about their performance for example, debriefing a teacher after a lesson observation.

    non-judgemental feedback – the technique of giving feedback to a person as evidence which is descriptive rather than as a series of judgements.

fellow – *see research fellow.*

financial administration – *see administration.*

flat structure – an organizational structure with few layers of management, in contrast to a hierarchic structure.

flexibility – an attitude which makes people ready to change and adapt the way they do things.

flexible learning (FL) – an approach to learning centred around self-instruction and small group tutorials.

flexitime – a system that allows employees to choose their own starting and finishing time within a broad range of available hours while still completing their contract.

force-field analysis – a technique for identifying the forces which restrain or drive an innovation forward.

forecasting – the attempt to predict future developments such as enrolments or financial needs.

Form 7 – an annual statistical report about pupil and staffing information which each school must return to the DFE.

formal organization – *see organization.*

formative evaluation – *see evaluation.*

formula funding – the process under Local Financial Management whereby schools receive a budget calculated according to a public formula established by each LEA, largely based on age-weighted pupil units, *see age-weighted pupil unit.*

forum – a meeting for the purpose of discussion or debate as in student/staff forum.

foundation subjects – *see subject.*

franchising – an economic partnership between educational institutions in the provision of courses, for example, where a part or the whole of the first year of a university degree course is delivered in a further education college on behalf of the university to the financial benefit of both institutions.

free period – the time during the school day allocated to teaching staff for preparation or marking; lesson when they do not have to teach in the classroom, *see non-contact time.*

full inspection – *see inspection.*

full-time employment – a job involving work on all working days throughout the year.

full-time equivalent (fte) – the calculation of staffing or student enrolment by adding together the amount of part-time staff or student time and describing it as if they were employed or attending full-time for example, 0.5 fte = a half-time member of staff.

funding – the provision of money in the form of loans or grants for a specific purpose.

grant funding – funding which does not have to be paid back.

loan funding – funding which must be paid back to the granting body.

seed-corn funding – funding provided to initiate a project which will subsequently be expected to become self-funding.

self-funding – the ability of an organization or person to fund themselves.

Funding Agency for Schools (FAS) – the national agency, a quango, which administers funds from the central government for Grant Maintained Schools.

further education – all types of post-school education apart from that given in higher education or degree-granting institutions.

G

GCSEs – the first public examinations – the General Certificate of Secondary Education – taken in usually up to ten subjects at the age of 16 at the end of compulsory schooling in England and Wales.

general assistant (GA) – an adult helper paid by the school who works with a teacher in a primary school classroom, providing support in organizing resources, listening to children read.

generalist – a person who is competent in several fields and is not highly specialized.

GNVQs – General National Vocational Qualifications which can be taken as alternatives to A-levels by students seeking a non-specialist technical and vocational education in years 12 and 13.

goal achievement/attainment – the degree to which purposes are realized.

goals – general statements of results one wishes to achieve.

governance – the legal process of governing or taking responsibility for an organization such as is exercised by Governing Bodies over schools or colleges.

Governing Body – the legally required board of lay and professional people who are elected or appointed to govern a school or college and have the final say over school policy and staffing appointments.

full Governing Body – the meeting of all members of the Governing Body when policy decisions have to be approved.

governor – a member of a school or college governing body.

Chair of Governors – the senior governor who acts as chairperson of the full Governing Body.

co-opted governor – a person appointed by elected governors to a governing body or sub-committee of governors because of some particular expertise.

lay governor – a member of a governing body who is not a professional educator.

parent governor – a parent elected by other parents to represent them for four years on a school's governing body.

teacher governor – a teacher elected by other teachers in a school to represent them on the governing body.

governors' sub-committee – one of several specialist committees into which a Governing Body is divided for the purpose of making recommendations to the full Governing Body for example, Finance, Staffing, Curriculum Sub-committees.

grant – a gift of money from a funding body to support study or research.

Education Support Grant (ESG) – a type of DFE grant for curriculum and staff development which was replaced by GEST.

Grant for Education Support and Training (GEST) – the method by which the DFE provides funding for curriculum, staff and management in-service training in schools and LEAs.

Local Education Authority Training Grants Scheme (LEATGS) – the DFE scheme for funding in-service training which was replaced by GEST.

mobility grant – money provided by employers to assist people to transfer their place of residence when changing jobs.

research grant – a non-repayable sum of money made available to an individual or an institution in order to carry out research and publish findings.

student grant – a non-repayable sum of money given by a Local Education Authority to a student to support study in further or higher education.

Green (consultation) paper – a discussion paper issued by the government at an early stage in the policy forming process and put out to interested parties for consultation.

group – several individuals brought together with or without a common purpose.

cultural minority group – *see ethnic minority group below.*

ethnic minority group – people with backgrounds deriving from cultures not indigenous to Britain but many of whom are born and raised in Britain for example, people of Asian, African or Caribbean heritage or refugees from anywhere in the world.

minority group – *see ethnic minority group above.*

mixed ability group – a group of pupils taught together who vary considerably in their academic capabilities.

mixed age group – a class of pupils of differing ages, usually in small rural primary schools.

mutual support group – a group of people who meet in order to offer one another help.

pressure group – a group of people who campaign to influence a particular policy, for example, to abolish corporal punishment.

target group – the group towards whom an innovation is directed and who will be expected to carry it out.

T-group – a training group in a social psychological programme designed to encourage the exploration of inner feelings and barriers to communication.

tutor group – the group of secondary school pupils who meet together usually each morning with their tutor for the purposes of registration and pastoral care.

working group – *see working party.*

group dynamics – the social processes which characterize all group interactions and are studied by social psychologists.

H

half-term – a school holiday usually one week long which comes mid-way through a school term.

hands-on experience – learning a specific skill by actually performing it in the real situation, often used with reference to learning computer skills.

harmonization – the process of standardizing regulations, laws and qualifications across different countries as in the European Union.

Hawthorne effect – the tendency of people involved in an observed experimental situation or innovation to produce uncharacteristically high performances which may not persist after the novel situation ceases.

head – a general term for a person in charge of an institution or sub-division of an institution.

> **head of department (HoD)** – the formal leader of an administrative unit within an educational institution.
>
> **head of faculty** – the leader of a group of departments or a particularly large department given faculty status in a secondary school, *see faculty*.
>
> **head of house (HoH)** – the teacher in charge of a mixed-age group of pupils assigned to a pastoral grouping or 'house' for the purpose of social activities or inter-house sports or other competitions.
>
> **head of lower/upper school** – the teachers with administrative responsibility for subdivisions of secondary schools as in lower school (Years 7–9) and upper school (Years 10–11).
>
> **head of year (HoY)** – the teacher or middle manager with responsibility for a team of tutors of all children of the same age band for example, Head of Year 7.

headmaster/headmistress – traditional terms for male and female headteachers, the latter term being increasingly preferred in state schools as a gender-neutral title for the head of a school.

Headmasters' Conference – the organization to which most of the headmasters of the most elite, fee-paying independent boys' 'public' schools belong.

headteacher – the senior professional within the hierarchy of a school, variously known as principal, school director, headmaster, headmistress.

headteacher appraisal – *see appraisal.*

Her Majesty's Inspector (HMI) – *see inspector.*

Her Majesty's Inspectorate (HMI) – an institution established in 1839 in Great Britain by the government to give advice to the Secretary of State and officials of the Department for Education, carry out inspections of institutions, prepare reports and documents for publication, liaise with local education authorities and provide in-service training courses for teachers.

hidden curriculum – *see curriculum.*

hierarchic structure – the classic top-down structure of a bureaucracy in which superordinates or line managers exercise authority over subordinates through a chain of command.

higher education – post-school education mainly involving advanced study leading to degrees and similar awards in universities, polytechnics and colleges of higher education.

Higher Education Funding Council for England (HEFCE) – one of the four regional funding councils for all higher education in the United Kingdom created in 1992 to increase central control of financing and quality assurance procedures.

high flier – a term used to describe a high achiever destined for success or promotion.

holistic – a concern for the wholeness of a person or situation when all aspects are considered and component parts are viewed as an integrated whole for example, holistic management development would consider psychological, social, situational, economic, political and cultural factors in interaction in developing 'the whole manager'.

home education – the provision of education in a child's own home, either by parents or a home tutor.

home tuition –

a) teaching provided by an LEA in the pupil's own home when illness or school phobia prevent attendance at school.

b) extra coaching in key examination subjects carried out by private tutors in a student's home and paid for by the parents.

homework – assignments of extra work to be completed at home outside normal school hours by students.

   homework diary – a diary issued by many secondary schools in which pupils record what homework they have been given in order to allow parents, tutors or year heads to monitor and support its completion.

   homework policy – a written statement of expectations about homework published by many schools.

   homework timetable – a schedule published for students by a school which sets out which evenings are allocated for the completion of homework in certain subjects.

honorary degree – *see degree.*

honours degree – *see degree.*

house – a mixed-age grouping of pupils organized in a school for the purposes of pastoral care and sporting or cultural competition against other houses in the school.

human relations movement – a period in the evolution of manage-ment theory in which an emphasis on the interpersonal factors in management challenged the prevailing assumptions of scientific management.

human resource management/development – *see management.*

I

ideology – a coherent set of inter-related beliefs which provide a basis for making sense of the world or guiding action for example, managerialism, progressive education.

image – the picture or impression which is projected by, or which one has of, a person or organization.

>**institutional image** – the reputation of a school or other edu-cational organization in the outside world.

>**occupational/professional image** – the status and reputation of a group of professionals such as teachers in the eyes of people in general.

implementation – the process of putting a plan into action.

improvement – an alteration or change which adds value or is for the better.

incentive – something, such as a reward or fear of punishment, which induces effort or increases motivation.

incentive allowance – *see allowance.*

inception report – the work plan of a major project produced in the first few weeks for the approval of the project management unit.

incompetence – the inability to perform a task to a minimum level of acceptability.

>**conscious incompetence** – being aware of one's inability to per-form to an acceptable standard.

>**unconscious incompetence** – being unaware of one's inability to perform to an acceptable standard.

independent school – *see school.*

individualization – the process of modifying a conventional class-taught programme of instruction into one designed for use by independent learners.

individualized learning – programmes of instruction designed for people to use independently without the need for interaction with other students or a teacher.

induction period – the early days of a person in a new job when they are supported in learning the new skills and acquiring the new understanding which they will need to become effective in their new role.

informal organization – *see organization.*

information – facts and data needed by members and clients of an organization.

    out-of-date information – facts and data which are no longer relevant.

    up-to-date information – facts and data which are current and relevant.

information technology (IT) – micro-electronic, telecommunications and computer hardware and software used to communicate and to record, process and publish data.

information technology office – the place in a large organization where IT services are located.

initial teacher education (ITE)/training (ITT) – *see pre-service teacher training.*

initiation – the launch of an initiative such as a planned change.

initiative –

a) the quality of showing enterprise or determination; a willingness to act independently.

b) a specific, usually short-term project, undertaken for the purpose of development for example, Technical and Vocational Education Initiative.

innovation – planned change which aims to improve materials, behaviours and beliefs.

    innovation fatigue/innovation overload – the perception that too many planned changes or reforms are being introduced simultaneously, leading to stress and overwork.

    multiple innovation – a process whereby many planned changes are implemented simultaneously.

innovator – a person who enjoys and seeks out opportunities to design and implement improvements or innovations.

input – resources or effort put into a system in order to help it function and achieve its purposes or output.

in-service education and training (INSET) – the process of updating teachers' professional skills or broadening their educational horizons after their initial qualification, for example, short courses, day conferences, secondments, distance learning materials.

non-disruptive INSET – INSET carried out at weekends or after school hours which does not disrupt the normal classroom teaching of teachers or require the use of substitute teachers to release teachers from their duties.

inspection – the process of visiting an institution in order to collect evidence for a systematic evaluation.

full inspection – the visit of a team of inspectors, representing a range of subjects or phase interests, to an educational institution in order to make an overall evaluation of standards and to produce a report.

inspection report – the report of each inspection by OFSTED teams of every educational institution which must be published for public scrutiny.

inspection team member – an OFSTED trained inspector who works in a team run by a Registered Inspector.

pre-inspection context and school indicator (PICSI) – a report compiled before a school OFSTED inspection to set the school in its local context, compare it with other schools and to identify more precise issues for inspection.

inspector – a post with responsibility for evaluating the performance of schools and teachers, for example, at national (HMI/OFSTED) and local (LEA) levels, with some specialization in inspecting subjects and/or phases (specific age groups of pupils).

Her Majesty's Inspector (HMI) – a national inspector with a monitoring function on behalf of the DFE which includes the evaluation of the work of the privatized OFSTED school inspection system.

independent inspector – a self-employed qualified inspector who is available to be hired by registered inspectors to work in OFSTED inspection teams.

lay inspector – the person with no professional background in education who is required by law to be a member of every OFSTED inspection team.

local education authority inspectors – evaluators employed by a local education authority to monitor educational standards in schools and colleges.

OFSTED inspector – an inspector employed to conduct an OFSTED inspection, *see Office for Standards in Education.*

Registered Inspector/'reggie' – the leader of a team of OFSTED inspectors.

Senior Chief Inspector – a post with overall responsibility for Her Majesty's Inspectorate's work which existed until September 1992.

institution – a formal organization with a specific purpose, identity, structure and title, for example, a school or university.

institutional development plan (IDP) – *see plan.*

institutionalization – the point at which the implementation of a planned change is completed and the new way of doing things becomes normal.

instruction – the formal presentation or imparting of knowledge.

instructor – a teacher mainly in further education, usually without formal teaching qualifications, who instructs in commercial or technical subjects.

instrument of government – the constitution of a school which sets out the duties of the governing body.

intake – the whole group of pupils or students arriving at the beginning of a new year.

    intake co-ordinator – the teacher or officer who is responsible for the management of the new students as they arrive.

    intake process – the activities needed to carry out the arrival of new students in an educational institution.

integrated day – a way of using time in a primary school which allows flexible patterns of individual study without dividing the timetable into formal subject lessons.

integration – the placing into normal schools of children with special educational needs who formerly were in special schools, *see mainstreaming.*

interaction – when two phenomena or people act upon one another.

inter-institutional – relating to relationships between two separate institutions.

interpersonal – those matters involving interaction or relationships between two or more individual people.

    interpersonal communications – the processes involved in conveying messages and meanings between people, including written, verbal and kinesic (body language) communication.

    interpersonal relations – the field of interest in all aspects of relationships between human beings.

interpersonal skills – those attributes and competencies which are employed in dealing with other people.

intervention – the process of taking action to modify or change a situation.

intervisitation – the exchange of visits between members of different organizations for the purposes of staff, management or curriculum development.

invigilation – the supervision of examinations in progress.

ipsative evaluation – *see evaluation.*

item bank – a collection of test questions from which tests can be made up.

J

job – the tasks which a person must carry out to fulfil their contract of employment; a specific task which needs to be done.

job analysis – examining the elements of a job in detail.

job description/specification – a list of key task areas in which the holder of a particular job is expected to achieve results.

job enhancement/enrichment – the process of adding to a person's job greater scope for personal achievement and recognition, more challenging and responsible work, and greater opportunity for advancement and growth.

job rotation – the practice in which employees, for example in a senior management team, take turns in doing each other's jobs in order to broaden their experience.

job satisfaction – the degree to which a person feels fulfilled and rewarded in their paid employment.

job security – the degree to which a person is guaranteed continuing employment.

job sharing – an arrangement whereby two or more part-time employees together cover a full-time equivalent job by working complementary hours, days or even weeks.

job specification – *see job description above.*

job swap – the exchange of jobs between two people in order to broaden their experience.

job title – the official label given to a post or postholder.

junior school – *see school.*

K

key results/task areas – clusters of related tasks which make up the elements of a job specification.

Key Stages – the four age bands of the National Curriculum in England and Wales into which schooling is divided between the ages five and sixteen.

kindergarten – a private school for children below five years old, the starting age for compulsory education.

L

law of education – legislation set out in Education Acts.

lay governor – *see governor.*

lay inspector – *see inspector.*

leader – a person who exercises power, authority and influence over a group derived both from his or her acceptance by the group, and his or her position in the formal organization.

leadership – the process of guiding followers in a certain direction in pursuit of a vision, mission or goals; making and implementing and evaluating policy.

    action-centred leadership – an approach to leadership which focuses on the satisfaction of three needs: task, group and individual.

    administrative leadership – the control exercised by leaders to ensure that resources and people are available to carry out an organization's purpose.

    charismatic leadership – an inspirational quality arising from a person's personality which motivates others to follow.

    cultural leadership – the process of creating a shared commitment to a set of values in line with an organization's vision and mission.

    educative leadership – the challenge of inspiring followers to engage in a continuous process of self and organizational development.

    instructional leadership – leadership in schools in which a head-teacher's activities are focused centrally on supporting teaching and learning in the classroom.

leadership style – the way a manager behaves in his or her roles as leader, for example, democratic, *laissez-faire*, autocratic, people-oriented, task-oriented.

peer-assisted leadership – a form of management development in which leaders such as headteachers are shadowed and given feedback about their performance by their peers for example, other headteachers.

situational leadership – the approach to leadership which stresses adjusting leadership behaviour to the level of experience of the followers or to the situation in hand, *see contingency theory.*

strategic leadership – the process of ensuring a long-term vision and plan for an organization and gaining the commitment of the followers to their implementation.

transactional leadership – an approach based on a bargain between followers, to work towards the achievement of organizational goals, and the leader, to ensure good working conditions and satisfy the needs of followers.

transformational/transformative leadership – a visionary approach to leadership in which leaders gain the commitment of followers to the extent that a high level of accomplishment becomes a moral imperative.

league tables – annually published lists, required by the Parents' Charter, of the overall results achieved in different schools in standardized tests and examinations, and other performance indicators such as truancy rates and school leaver destinations, in order to allow comparisons to be made between schools.

learning organization – *see organization.*

lecturer – a teacher in a higher or further education institution.

principal lecturer – a teacher in a higher education institution who has been promoted to a senior rank in that role.

senior lecturer – a teacher in a higher or further education institution who has earned promotion and receives a higher salary than a lecturer.

leisure time activity – pursuits such as hobbies, sport or social activities which people choose to do in their own time.

lesson observation – the observation of teachers in the classroom by other teachers in order to give them feedback about their performance or to appraise their competence.

lesson observation proforma (LOP) – the document produced by an OFSTED inspector which uses specified criteria against which to grade the standard of a teacher's lesson which has been observed during an inspection of the school; criteria include content, standard of pupil achievement, quality of learning and teaching.

level descriptions – the actual statements which describe levels of attainment within each attainment target in the National Curriculum.

levels of attainment – the technical term used in the National Curriculum for the eight levels of skills and knowledge which define a pupil's mastery of an attainment target within a subject.

liaison officer – *see officer.*

liabilities – debts which are owed to other persons or organizations.

licensed teacher – a teacher who is trained in a school over a one year period with the support of the local education authority, as opposed to an institute of higher education.

life-long education – the principle that education in a variety of forms such as community, adult or extra-mural education, should continue to be an entitlement throughout life.

line management – *see management.*

link course – *see course.*

loans – grants of money which have to be repaid, as in low-interest student loans introduced by the 1990 Student Loans Act.

Local Education Authority (LEA) – the basic unit for administering schools in Britain, managed by an Education Committee of locally elected politicians and the permanent staff of local government administrators.

local education authority inspectors – *see inspector.*

Local Financial Management (LFM) – the delegation of responsibility for budget management from LEAs to schools.

local management of schools (LMS) – *see management.*

locus of control – a psychological term meaning where people see the location of the power to determine their lives: either internally or outside themselves.

London allowance – *see allowance.*

long course – *see course.*

loosely coupled organization – *see organization.*

M

magnet school – *see school.*

main professional grade – the basic salary grade for teachers who have no management responsibilities or incentive allowances, now called standard national scale.

mainstreaming – an American term for placing pupils with special educational needs into regular (mainstream) schools.

maintenance grant – an LEA grant to post-16 students to cover living costs as opposed to educational fees.

management –

a) the structures for and process of planning, co-ordinating and directing the activities of people, departments or organizations; getting things done with and through other people.

b) the individual or group of individuals who manage an organization.

    boundary management – the task of managing relationships with people, agencies and other organizations external to the institution, for example, a school's links with the LEA, local community or other schools.

    creative management – the use of original and divergent thinking in achieving goals with and through other people.

    crisis management – a practice that seeks to deal with innovations, shortcomings and failures through reaction rather than planning, often involving drastic measures.

    financial management – the creation of financial policy and plans and assuring their implementation and evaluation.

    human resource management/development – a process of managing and developing all personnel in an organization in order better to achieve organizational goals.

    line management – the chain of authority in formal hierarchies consisting of managers and their subordinates.

    local management of schools (LMS) – a term which describes in the UK, the delegation of responsibility for school budgeting and staff appointment from the LEA to each individual school's governing body and senior management team.

    management by exceptions – the practice of focusing attention primarily on errors or on unintended results.

    management by objectives (MBO) – a process whereby detailed desired outcomes or objectives are established and progress in achieving them is systematically monitored.

management by walking around (MBWA) – an approach to communicating with personnel and getting feedback from them in the workplace by talking, asking questions, and learning about operations on a first-hand basis.

management functions – the basic activities required of managers in the performance of their jobs such as policy making, planning, implementing and evaluating.

management guru – a writer of best-selling management books who becomes famous as a lecturer and trainer in management.

management information system (MIS) – a specific data-processing system that is designed to provide management and supervisory personnel with access to current information for example about student enrolment, examination results or budgets.

management techniques – specific skills and procedures used in achieving results in organizations for example, planning, critical path analysis, team-building.

open management – a style of management in which the assumptions, values and budget considerations underlying policy making are made clear and shared throughout an organization.

participative management – an approach to management which invites widespread participation in decision-making.

school-based management – the process of managing delegated budgets and decision-making within relatively autonomous schools.

scientific management – an approach to management theory associated initially with Frederick 'Speedy' Taylor which emphasizes the application of scientific methods to the tasks of management, for example, time and motion studies to increase worker productivity.

senior management – the people responsible for strategic leadership of a whole organization.

stress management – the process of creating the procedures, interpersonal relationships and conditions in which damaging stress is avoided or kept to a minimum.

time management – the planning and implementation of the optimum use of time by setting work priorities, identifying tasks which can be delegated and ensuring that time is not wasted on non-productive activities.

top management – *see senior management above.*

total quality management (TQM) – an approach to management which focuses on the quality of services and products to internal and external 'customers' at every level of the organization at all times, seeking to eliminate errors and satisfy fully, clearly stated and agreed customer requirements at the lowest possible cost.

Management Charter Initiative (MCI) – a national initiative to define and classify the competencies required by managers in all occupational sectors, including education and training, as a basis for assessing and raising standards.

management development plan – *see plan.*

manager – an individual responsible for the planning, co-ordination and direction of people, a department, or an organization.

line manager – an employee's immediate superior in a hierarchic organization.

middle manager – a term increasingly used to describe heads of faculty, departments or years in secondary schools who are responsible to the Senior Management Team (SMT).

senior manager – a member of the Senior Management Team for example, in a school, usually the head, deputy heads and senior teachers.

top manager – *see senior manager above.*

managerial grid – a technique for measuring a manager's leadership style in terms of concern for people and concern for tasks.

managerial insight – the capacity to identify and be sensitive to the problems of getting things done with and through other people.

managerialism – the assumption that management is the solution to many organizational problems; often a pejorative term directed at those who see management as an end rather than means, particularly in the publicly funded services.

managerial performance – the extent to which a manager achieves intended results with and through other people.

managerial roles – the specified set of activities and expectations that define the part played by the manager in the organization.

managerial tasks – items of work which need to be accomplished in order to pursue organizational purposes, for example, decision making (collective, individual), managing meetings, managing stress (reducing level of stress), performing administrative work.

mandatory award – the compulsory award of a grant by LEAs to a student based on national criteria of eligibility.

Masters degree – higher degree obtained after one or two years of study beyond Bachelors degree level by means of research and sometimes taught modules.

mature student – a student who enters higher education after a break of some years from full-time study who can sometimes be exempted from normal entry qualifications.

MBO *see management by objectives.*

mean – a statistical term for 'average'.

    Aristotelian golden mean – finding a path between two extreme positions.

media resources – equipment, both hardware and software, used to support teaching for example, overhead projectors, television, CD-ROM.

media resources officer – *see officer.*

mentor – an experienced colleague who provides systematic professional advice and support to a less experienced colleague.

mentoring – a coaching relationship offered by a more experienced to a less experienced colleague in order to improve their professional performance.

message – the content of a communication.

    decode a message – to interpret a signal or communication in order to understand its surface or deeper meaning.

    encode a message – to translate it into a signal or signals.

micropolitics – the subtle use of power and influence in an organization to achieve purposes for example, building informal coalitions or pressure groups, 'massaging' minutes which record decisions made at meetings.

middle manager – *see manager.*

milieu – the physical or social surroundings or climate of an organization.

mind map – a flow diagram of key words used in creative note making, brainstorming or planning.

Minister of Education – a politician who is responsible for the national education system, usually alone, but in England and Wales, with the assistance of junior ministers, *see Secretary of State for Education.*

Ministry of Education – that part of a national government which is responsible for the education system of the country, called in England and Wales, the Department for Education – DFE (formerly Department for Education and Science – DES).

minority group – *see group*.

mission – the values and long term goals of an organization usually written down as a 'mission statement' to guide strategic thinking.

    mission statement – a short written description of the overall philosophy, purposes, vision or mission of an organization.

mixed ability group – *see group*.

mixed age classes – classes containing pupils of differing ages from more than one year group.

mobilization – the act of motivating and moving people into action to implement policies.

modelling behaviour – the demonstration by a coach or mentor of effective ways of performing.

modularization – the process of converting a series of courses into modules.

module – a unit of learning within a programme to which a number of credit points are attached depending on the module's length in order to be accumulated towards a qualification for example, a Masters degree programme requires the accumulation of 120 credits which could be earned by completing eight 10-credit modules plus a 40-credit dissertation.

monitoring – the process of checking how accurately plans are being implemented.

    self-monitoring – the monitoring of one's own performance without the involvement of outsiders.

monitoring system – the procedures established for checking the implementation of plans.

morale – the degree of well-being felt by an individual, members of an organization or profession.

motivation –

a) the process of encouraging people to perform.

b) a person's inclination towards action.

    extrinsic motivation – the stimulus to action coming from outside a person.

    intrinsic motivation – the inclination towards action arising from within, *see self-motivation below*.

    self-motivation – the capacity for committing oneself to action without the need for external stimuli or rewards.

    unconscious motivation – motivation evident from a person's pattern of behaviour but of which that person is not aware.

motivational hygiene theory – a theory which identifies conditions of a job that dissatisfy employees when they are not present (hygiene factors – salary, job security) and job conditions that lead to high levels of satisfaction when present (motivators – achievement, growth); factors which appear to be independent of one another.

motivational needs – psychological and physical factors which affect thinking and behaviour, for example, needs for self-actualization, esteem, belonging, security, survival.

motivator – a person or condition which encourages people to act.

municipal – a term relating to the local government of a city or urban district.

Murphy's Laws – popular axioms emphasizing the difficulties of managerial life: nothing is as simple as it seems; everything takes longer than you think; if anything can go wrong it will.

mutual observation – the professional development activity in which colleagues take turns in observing one another at work in order to provide feedback for example, mutual lesson observation between teachers.

N

National Curriculum – *see curriculum.*

needs – essential requirements which must be satisfied.

    needs analysis/assessment/identification – the procedures for discovering what people, institutions or systems require as a prelude to planning development programmes.

    needs theory – the hierarchy of physiological and emotional needs outlined by Maslow: basic, safety, belonging, esteem and self-actualization, *see motivational needs.*

negotiation – the process of discussion which attempts to reach agreement between various parties who often have conflicting interests and needs.

network – a non-hierarchic organization of people or institutions who relate to and communicate with one another for some shared purpose.

networking – the process of building relationships and communication between members of a network.

neuro-linguistic programming (NLP) – an approach to training, increasingly used in management development, involving the use of goal-setting, visualization, positive thinking and other psychological techniques derived from studies of high performing people.

newly qualified teacher (NQT) – *see teacher.*

noise – anything which impedes or interferes with a message, and was not intended by the sender.

non-contact time – those lessons within a school timetable when teachers do not have to be in classrooms with pupils or students and therefore are free to prepare lessons, mark books, keep records.

non-judgemental – the technique of communicating without making judgements, *see feedback.*

non-statutory guidance – those suggestions in the statutory orders relating to the National Curriculum which are not compulsory but which offer ideas about teaching content which teachers might wish to use.

non-teaching staff – *see ancillary staff.*

norm – a standard, model or pattern regarded as typical.

norm-referenced test – *see test.*

novelty – an event, experience or item which is unexpected, new or original.

O

objectives – specific statements of identifiable results one wishes to achieve.

  behavioural objectives – describing results in terms of observable actions which learners are able to perform.

Office for Standards in Education (OFSTED) – since 1992, an independent office of Her Majesty's Chief Inspector of Schools which provides advice to the government on educational matters and which established and monitors the privatized, independent inspection by registered and OFSTED trained inspectors, of schools, Colleges of Further Education and Initial Teacher Training Institutions.

officer – a position in an administrative hierarchy.

Chief Education Officer (CEO) – sometimes called Director of Education, the principal non-elected administrator of a Local Education Authority who is the senior local government official responsible to the elected education committee.

Deputy Chief Education Officer – a local government administrator or officer second-in-charge of a Local Education Authority.

education officer – a local government official with administrative (not inspection or advisory) responsibilities for education, for example, finance, school buildings, transport.

education welfare officer (EWO) – an employee of a local education authority who deals with school-related social problems experienced by pupils and their families such as truancy.

examinations officer – the person in a secondary school who takes responsibility for the administration of public examinations.

health and safety officer – the person required by law to monitor compliance with health and safety regulations in the work place.

liaison officer – an official who acts as a link between two organizations or departments within an organization.

media resources officer – the person in charge of media resources.

off-site training – *see training.*

off-the-job training – *see training.*

O-level – the former ordinary level of the General Certificate of Education examination taken by most pupils at the age of 16 and now replaced by the GCSE examination.

one-off training – seeing training as a single event rather than as a continuing process of development.

one-to-one support – a situation in which one person has an individual counsellor, coach or mentor to assist in counselling or professional development.

one-way communication – *see communication.*

on-site training – *see training.*

on-the-job experience – the learning obtained simply by doing a job for a period of time, without or in addition to any formal training.

on-the-job training – *see training.*

open admission/access – the freedom to enter an education programme with no restrictions such as entry qualifications.

Open College – *see college.*

open day – a public relations day on which parents and members of the local community are invited to visit a school in order to find out how it works.

open enrolment – *see enrolment.*

open evening – *see parents' evening.*

open management – *see management.*

Open Tech – an organization set up in 1981 with government sponsorship to promote adult retraining in the area of technology.

Open University – a distance learning university established in England in 1969 whose students benefit from an open admissions policy and learn by means of print, radio and television media supported by a regional tutoring network.

opting out – the process whereby a school leaves the administrative control of a local education authority to become a Grant Maintained School.

options – *see subject option.*

organic structure – an organization design characterized by a decentralized hierarchy, flexible work procedures, and democratic leadership, with informal and open communication, as distinct from a formal, inflexible, 'mechanistic' bureaucracy.

organigram/organizational flow chart – a diagram which sets out the roles and relationships of key individuals, teams and departments within an organization.

organization – a social unit or place in which people work together towards specific purposes, usually with some division of labour.

　formal organization – a tightly structured organization based on clearly set out roles, jobs and procedures, often with little flexibility in delegation of authority and assignment of tasks and responsibilities.

　informal organization – a flexibly structured organization, free of rigid rules for activity and authority; sometimes a covert group in a school staff room which seeks to influence policy.

　learning organization – an organization in which reflective practice and a search for continuous improvement are encouraged resulting in an in-built capacity for self-transformation.

　loosely coupled organization – an organization in which much autonomy accrues to sub-groups and individuals, making it difficult for senior management to implement its policies.

organizational – relating to an organization.

organizational change – *see change.*

organizational climate – the quality of relationships between members of an organization including their morale, job satisfaction, degree of involvement.

organizational culture – the values, norms and beliefs which characterize organizations and are symbolized through patterns of interaction, dress, speech and shared by all members or, as sub-cultures, by some groups of members.

organizational development – *see development.*

organizational level – the position of members in an organizational hierarchy for example, top level – concerned with setting goals and strategic planning; middle level – concerned with co-ordinating and integrating work performance.

organizational structure – the formally defined framework of roles, lines of authority and procedures designed to ensure the achievement of an organization's tasks.

outcome – the product or end-result of a process or project.

outdoor training – *see training.*

output – a term from systems theory which represents outcome from a system; *see outcome.*

outreach – the process whereby teachers move out into the community to take education to both young and adult people who are disinclined to pursue formal education.

overload – the state of carrying a load which is too great for the person or system to bear.

Oxbridge – a conflation of the names of Oxford and Cambridge Universities to provide a collective noun.

P

paradigm – a set of assumptions or perspectives which provide a dominant view of reality at any given time but which can change suddenly with some new breakthrough in understanding for example, the scientific management paradigm.

parent power – the ability of parents to influence school policy and practice which has been increasing in recent years due to government policy.

Parents' Charter – a document setting out parents' rights and responsibilities with respect to the education of their children published in 1991 as part of the government's Citizens' Charter.

parents' evening – an evening set aside by teachers for parents to visit the school in order to discuss the progress of their children.

participative management – *see management.*

part-time – an employee employed for only part of a working week.

passivity – the quality of not reacting or taking initiative.

pass rate – the proportion of candidates who succeed in a test or examination.

pastoral care – the provision of support in schools for pupils' welfare through a system of tutor groups, houses or years.

    pastoral care staff – teachers who, in addition to teaching, provide support for the welfare of pupils and act as their tutor.

pay spine – the graduated scale of teachers' salaries and incentive allowances from which the national system of teachers' pay is constructed.

pedagogue – an archaic term for a teacher of the young.

pedagogy – the art or science of teaching children.

peer – a person of similar role and status.

    peer-assisted leadership – *see leadership.*

    peer coaching – the process of receiving feedback about performance from people of the same level and occupation.

    peer group – a group of equals such as a year group in a school.

    peer teaching – the practice of having pupils teach other pupils.

performance appraisal – *see appraisal.*

performance indicators – precise, often measurable, descriptions of outcomes which one aims to achieve.

performance related pay (PRP) – a system whereby salaries or wages are based on an appraisal of the merit of the employee's contribution to the organization.

performance tables – published statistics relating to a school's examination and National Curriculum test results, truancy rates and school leaver destinations.

performance targets – *see performance indicators.*

peripatetic teacher – *see teacher.*

personal fulfilment – the sense of having reached one's personal goals, a high sense of individual efficacy.

personnel – the staff employed by an organization.

PERT (Programme Evaluation and Review Technique) – a method used for rational planning and evaluation.

phase – the stage of formal education through which a person passes that is, primary, secondary, tertiary.

pilot scheme/school – a trial of a new initiative on a limited basis in selected schools.

placement – the allocation of someone to a particular situation or activity.

  industrial placement – the opportunity given to some managers in schools to spend a short time in an industrial enterprise to observe how it is managed.

  teacher placement – allocating teachers to specific schools.

plan – a set of goals and steps intended to achieve them.

  action plan – a plan intended for rapid implementation, often used to provide a focus for the outcome of a meeting or workshop.

  development plan – a plan for improving an institution, which reviews the current situation, sets targets and states how these are to be achieved and monitored.

  institutional development plan (IDP) – *see development plan above and school development plan below.*

  long-term plan – upwards of three years.

  management development plan – a plan produced in order to improve the quality of management structures, processes and personnel in an organization.

  medium-term plan – for one to three years.

  open plan – a school building, usually at primary school level, in which several classes of pupils with their teachers share the same large open room when being taught.

  rolling plan – a plan which is modified on a regular basis.

  school development plan (SDP) – a plan drawn up by a school, usually for a period of three years, as a means of managing school improvement and imposed innovations.

  short-term plan – a plan made for up to one year.

  work plan – *see action plan above.*

planned change – *see change.*

planning – imagining the desired future and the steps needed to achieve it.

  action planning – a tautology, perhaps more accurately meaning short-term planning, which gives an added sense of determination to implement the plan.

collaborative planning – a process in which a team of people work very closely together to produce a plan for which they all subsequently feel responsible.

evolutionary planning – an approach which accepts that original plans will have to be adjusted during their implementation.

future-based planning – a procedure for planning which starts with visualizing the desired future as if it already existed and then working backwards, step by step to the present in order to work out the necessary resources and events to achieve the vision.

operational planning – the process of arranging specific, short-term, everyday activities.

rational planning – the assumption that plans can actually be implemented faithfully according to an original design ignoring the inevitability of unforeseen events and human error.

strategic planning – working out long-term goals (vision, mission) and the means of achieving them.

policy – a set of principles or purposes to justify and guide the process of planning.

educational policy – the principles and goals set out by central and local governments to be applied to the educational systems which they govern.

national policy – the policy of the government of a country.

policy alternatives – a variety of options for change in policy usually generated as part of a policy review.

policy implementation – the process of turning policy into action.

policy maker – a person who takes part in the decisions relating to the principles and goals of an organization.

policy making – the process of formulating policy.

polytechnic – a higher education institution offering technical, professional and vocational courses and awards. In Britain these became universities in 1993.

portfolio – a collection of documents produced by a student or teacher for the purpose of demonstrating their achievements and capabilities.

position/post – a job within an organization to which an individual is formally appointed.

positive discrimination – giving special privileges or resources to disadvantaged groups.

post-compulsory education – education beyond the minimum school leaving age of sixteen.

post-graduate – a person or course beyond the level of a Bachelors or first degree.

Post-graduate Certificate of Education (PGCE) – the award for a one year course of professional preparation to be a teacher which is taken by graduates with degrees in subjects other than education.

potential schools' budget – *see budget.*

power – the ability to exercise control of people and resources.

PPBS (Planning, Programming, Budgeting System) – a long range planning procedure in which the costs and benefits of alternative plans are analysed in determining budgets.

practice –
a) the work performed by a practitioner.
b) the actuality of events as they occur (as opposed to theory).

practitioner – a person who practises a profession for example, a teacher or a doctor.

   reflective practitioner – a professional who adopts an analytical stance to her/his own performance and situation in order to improve both.

prefect – a special post of responsibility for senior pupils in schools which has largely died out in state schools in recent years, though is still common in independent schools.

pre-inspection context and school indicators (PICSI) – *see inspection.*

pre-school education – all types of educational provision for children under the age of five, before the start of compulsory education, including playgroups, kindergarten, nursery education.

pre-service teacher training – *see training.*

pre-vocational education – the provision in secondary schools of courses designed to prepare students for the world of work, or to follow vocational courses.

Principal –
a) in Great Britain the head of a further education institution and certain types of school.
b) in the USA, and several other countries, a term for school headteacher.

principal lecturer – *see lecturer.*

Private Finance Initiative (PI) – a government initiative launched in 1992 to promote partnership between public and private sectors, including education, on a commercial basis.

privatization – the transfer of ownership of public sector organizations into private hands.

proactive – an assertive attitude, typical of dynamic leaders, which leads them to take initiatives and not wait for things to happen.

probationary year – the first year of teaching during which a teacher used to be assessed on-the-job before being regarded as fully qualified to practise as a teacher.

productivity – the ratio of what is produced to what is needed to produce it, a concept difficult to apply, but increasingly being examined, in education where it would require learning outcomes to be compared with teaching inputs, *see value-added*.

professional – a member of an occupation requiring lengthy education, a sense of vocation and the exercise of judgement in the interest of clients as an overriding value.

    professional association – the equivalent of a trade union for members of a profession for example, NASUWT, NAHT, NATFHE, AUT.

    professional development/growth – *see development*.

    professional journal – a written record of reflections about daily work experiences which is used as a basis for self-development.

professionalism – the quality and attitude of serving one's clients to the best of one's ability.

professionality – the exercise of professional skills.

professionalization – the process of increasing the status of an occupational group by toughening the entry qualifications, creating professional associations and so on.

professor – the highest rank of lecturer in a university.

    assistant professor – an American term for lecturer.

    associate professor – an American term for senior lecturer.

    visiting professor – a professor from another university or country who spends a period of time lecturing or doing research on a temporary attachment to a university.

profile component – a group of attainment targets within a subject in the National Curriculum.

programme – a series of courses combined together into a coherent learning experience for example, Masters degree programme.

attachment programme – a learning experience provided for a foreign visitor, a seconded professional or groups of such people a higher education institution.

exchange programme – an arrangement whereby two or more scholars or students change places, usually between countries.

programme of study – the outline of the aims and content of a particular course.

project – a special enterprise, usually of short duration, designed to make improvements or achieve specific goals.

project design – the first stage of a project in which a detailed plan is created.

project evaluation – the process of gathering evidence in order to judge whether project goals have been met.

project implementation – the phase of a project in which the plan is carried out and ideas are turned into action.

project management unit (PMU) – the steering group to whom the managers of a project are accountable.

promotion – the achievement of being selected for and moving to a job of higher status and pay.

prospectus – a booklet or brochure which outlines the aims and programmes and courses offered by an educational institution for the purpose of marketing.

Pro-vice-chancellor – a senior academic and manager in a university who assists the Vice-chancellor in running the institution, often taking responsibility for a particular section of the organization.

psychological service – the provision by LEAs of the services of educational psychologists to support the schools, and in particular, children with learning or behavioural difficulties.

public expenditure – that part of the national budget arising from taxation which is spent by central and local governments or publicly owned institutions.

public expenditure for education – the proportion of public spending dedicated to the education system.

public sector – that part of the economy not in private ownership, funded by government from taxation for example, education, health or welfare services.

pupil – a young person, usually in primary or secondary school, who is engaged in compulsory education.

delinquent pupil – a pupil whose behaviour is causing major problems in school.

EBD pupil – a pupil with special educational and behavioural difficulties.

SEN pupil – a pupil with special educational needs, *see special educational needs.*

statemented pupil – a pupil who has been assessed as needing additional resources to help overcome learning difficulties.

pupil attendance – the percentage of pupils who turn up to school in a given period of compulsory schooling.

pupil council – *see student council.*

pupil/student monitoring system – the procedures used to keep track of pupils' progress through school and their achievements.

pupil-teacher ratio – the number of pupils in a school or system in relation to the number of teachers for example, 1 teacher:18 pupils.

purposes – *see goals.*

Q

qualitative evaluation/research – *see evaluation.*

quality – the fitness for purpose of an object, person, performance or organization; the extent to which goals or standards are attained.

quality assessment – the process of measuring the value of an organization's people, processes and performance.

quality assurance – the guarantee that procedures are in place and available with which to assess performance.

quality audit – the formal review, usually by outside assessors, of the performance and provision of a university or department within a university.

quality circle – a work-based group meeting where colleagues explore together ways of improving the quality of their work.

quality control – the procedures used to ensure that standards of performance or production are maintained.

quango – the acronym standing for 'quasi-autonomous non-governmental organization' meaning an advisory or regulatory body which is appointed by government rather than elected but which is given a degree of independence from government control.

quantitative evaluation/research – *see evaluation.*

R

rate capping – the policy of central government to place a limit on the amount of local taxes (rates) which local government can raise in order to fund education and other services.

rate of failure – the proportion of people or products out of a total population attempting to achieve a minimum standard which fails to do so.

rates – local taxes paid to local government districts or counties.

rational planning model – a diagram which sets out the logical steps in management often in the form of a cycle, for example moving from needs to policy and on to planning, implementation and evaluation, thereby returning to needs.

reader – a university lecturer whose rank falls between that of senior lecturer and professor.

reception classes – groups of pupils who are at the start of their compulsory schooling and are taught together by one or more teachers.

reconciliation to change – *see change.*

record-keeping – records of all pupils' academic progress, including the results of National Curriculum assessment at age 7, 11, 14 and 16.

record of achievement (RoA) – a method of summarizing a pupil's attainments and activities in school in the form of a portfolio, so that they can be passed on from teacher to teacher, from school to school or on to employers.

recruitment – the process of hiring new employees.

recurrent education – *see continuing education.*

redbrick university – a term which distinguishes newer universities from Oxbridge.

redeployment – voluntary or compulsory transfer of staff to another teaching post in a different school, usually because of falling rolls in the original school.

redundancy – the dismissal of an employee, usually with a financial settlement, when that employee is no longer needed.

    compulsory redundancy – when an employee has no choice about being made redundant.

    voluntary redundancy – when an employee accepts an offer to be made redundant.

reflective practitioner – *see practitioner.*

reform – literally to change the form of something, the broad term for any significant planned innovation designed to improve a system, institution, group or individual.

educational reform – those broad attempts to change the educational system and its institutions through legislation, initiatives, projects, usually on a scale involving many institutions.

refresher course – *see course.*

registered inspector/'reggie' – *see inspector.*

registrar – a senior administrator in a university or college with responsibility for student registration, examinations and records.

registration –

a) the act of enrolling a person onto a course.

b) the daily recording of pupils' attendance in a school register.

regulations – rules designed to govern behaviour within an organization.

reification – the tendency to treat concepts as if they had a life or mind of their own, for example, 'the school believes that . . .'

release – to free from normal duties.

block release – the freeing of workers for blocks of time from their normal jobs in order to engage in formal study.

day release – the freeing of workers from their jobs to attend vocational education activities.

teacher release – covering the work of teachers so that they can take part in in-service education activities.

remedial teaching – specialist teaching for pupils with learning difficulties or special educational needs.

remediation – providing remedies or special support to overcome shortcomings or below standard performance.

report – the written summary of pupil progress sent by tutors to parents, usually each term, and discussed at parents' evenings.

requirements – those responsibilities or obligations which are compulsory as a result of a contract or an agreement.

research and development (R and D) – a style of applied research activity which focuses on practical outcomes in order to lead to improvements in the process or product which is the object of the research.

research fellow – a temporary or permanent post in an institution of higher education of similar status to a lecturer, but primarily for the purpose of research rather than teaching.

research grant – *see grant.*

research project – a systematic enquiry, usually short-term, designed to produce new knowledge or to test new materials or methods and produce a report, academic publication or dissertation.

residential care – the provision by LEAs of a place in which to live and be educated for young people in need.

resistance to change – *see change.*

resource acquisition – the act of finding and obtaining the resources required to implement plans.

resource allocation – decisions relating to how available resources will be used.

    resource allocation formula – the formula used by local education authorities to determine how much money will be delegated to each school from the general schools' budget.

resource centre – the room or complex of rooms located either in schools, in further and higher education institutions or LEAs to store books, non-book materials and audio-visual software and to provide facilities for producing learning materials.

resources – human labour, information, materials, money and time available for running an organization and pursuing its goals.

responsibilities – tasks or obligations for which an individual or organization is responsible.

responsiveness – the sensitivity towards, and ability to cater for, the needs of people and situations.

restraining forces – *see force-field analysis.*

restructuring – the process of reorganizing an education system including the delegation of budgets from local authorities to the schools.

revenue – all forms of income, grants and gifts available for financing an organization.

review – a systematic and thorough evaluation.

reviewee – a person who is the subject of a review.

reviewer – a person who carries out a review.

rising fives – children who are not yet five years old but who are allowed to enrol in primary school reception classes to start their compulsory education.

role – the part one is expected or appointed or undertakes to play within a social or work situation.

    role expectations – the pressure to perform in a certain way which arises from what people in the work place (role set) expect someone to do.

role model – a person whose behaviour others aspire to emulate or copy.

role set – the group of people in a work situation whose expectations influence the behaviour of a person in a particular role.

roll – the list of all pupils enrolled in a school or class.

declining/falling rolls – a situation in which the number of pupils or students entering or staying in an educational institution is going down.

increasing/rising rolls – a situation in which the number of pupils or students entering or staying in an educational institution is becoming larger.

S

sabbatical – a period of paid leave for private study or research, varying in length from one term to one year, commonly available in higher education institutions.

sandwich course – *see course.*

schedule – a timetable outlining a sequence of events.

scholarship –

a) an award of money to assist a student taking a higher education course based on an assessment of high potential, sometimes following success in an entrance examination.

b) a demonstrably high standard of academic performance.

school –

a) an institution for educating young people.

b) a sub-unit within a higher educational institution, for example, School of Education, School of Music.

alternative school – a private school, usually based on radical principles, established to provide an education outside that provided by the public authorities or conventional private schools.

autonomous school – a school which is self-governing and self-managing.

boarding school – a type of school in which pupils live as residents during term-time.

community school – a type of school based on a concept of education which seeks to promote educational activities for members of the local community, regardless of age, and provides access to school facilities beyond normal school opening hours.

comprehensive school – a non-selective secondary school, originally drawing pupils from a defined catchment area, which takes pupils of all abilities and offers them a full, comprehensive range of courses.

effective school – a school which adds the greatest value in terms of pupil learning in relation to the inputs of resources; a term introduced in the 1980s as a result of a number of studies which showed that the performance of children from similar backgrounds differed according to factors within the schools.

elementary school –
a) a type of school in Great Britain prior to 1944 in which children from 5 to 14 years of age were educated.
b) a term still used in the USA to mean primary school.

free school – a type of private school popular in the 1960s, usually offering a pupil-centred, 'freer' curriculum for parents interested in an alternative education for their children, particularly those who make little progress in state schools.

grammar school – a selective school, usually for 11–18-year-olds of higher than average academic ability, most of whom are destined for a higher academic education.

grant maintained school (GMS) – a school which has opted out of Local Education Authority control and receives its budget direct from the national government through the Funding Agency for Schools (FAS).

high school – an American term for secondary school which is occasionally used in the UK.

independent school – a type of school not in receipt of grants from government or Local Education Authorities, depending instead on fees from parents.

infants school – the first two years of primary school for pupils aged 5–7.

junior school – a type of school which caters for children between the ages of 7 and 11.

lower school/upper school – subdivisions of secondary schools for pastoral purposes, for example, 11–14 age group – lower school; 15–18 age group – upper school.

magnet school – an American term for secondary schools which specialize in particular areas of the curriculum such as the performing arts or technology and which provided the inspiration for the creation in Britain of city technology colleges and technology colleges.

mainstream school – a non-specialist or normal school with a typical range of courses and students.

maintained school – a type of school financed from public taxes, both national and local, that is, not a private school.

middle school – schools for the age range 10 or 11 to 13 or 14 found in a small number of LEAs.

nursery school/kindergarten – a pre-school for children under the age of 5.

preparatory school – a private school in the Incorporated Association of Preparatory Schools, where children are prepared for entry into independent schools.

primary school – a type of school which caters for children between the ages of 5–11 (includes both infant and junior schools).

public school – a term confusingly used to mean a private or independent school.

secondary modern school – a school, of which few now remain, established by the 1944 Education Act, which takes pupils aged 11–16 not selected for grammar schools.

secondary school – a school for children over the age of 11 (who have finished their primary school education) where they remain until the compulsory school leaving age of 16, or two or three years beyond that.

self-developing school – a school which takes responsibility for running its own staff development and school improvement programme.

self-governing school – a school such as a grant maintained or private school whose governing body is free from any form of control from an LEA.

self-managing school – a school where senior staff and governors are responsible for managing budgets and decisions which were formerly managed by Local Education Authorities but are now delegated.

special school – a type of school provided for groups of children who have special educational needs, for example, schools for emotionally and behaviourally disturbed, partial hearing, blind, physically disabled pupils.

split site school – a school which operates in two different locations or campuses, usually due to the amalgamation of two formerly separate schools.

state school – a school financed by the state and not privately.

upper school – *see lower school above.*

voluntary-aided school – a school maintained and 85 per cent funded by the LEA but in which two-thirds of the governors are appointed by a voluntary, usually a church, organization and who control the admission of pupils and the type of religious education taught.

voluntary-controlled school – originally a church-owned school now totally funded by the LEA which appoints two-thirds of the governing body.

school-based budget – *see budget.*

school-based INSET/staff development – development activities for staff carried out on the school site.

school-based management – *see management.*

school-based management training – *see training.*

school catchment area – *see catchment area.*

school-centred management training – *see training.*

school-centred staff development – development activities focused on the needs of the school, usually with participants from one school which can be carried out either on-site or away from the school.

school climate – the prevailing character of interpersonal and social relationships which can be detected in a school.

school–community relations – the degree and quality of interaction between a school and its surrounding local community.

school council – a body of pupils who are either elected or nominated within a school to express views on school matters and whose terms of reference are normally laid down by the headteacher and staff.

school culture – the unique values, rituals, symbols, beliefs, traditions, ways of doing things which distinguish one school from another.

School Curriculum and Assessment Authority – the government appointed agency which designs the national school curriculum and standardized tests administered at ages 7, 11 and 14.

school day – the length of time a school is open for pupils during which attendance is compulsory.

school development plan (SDP) – *see plan.*

school effectiveness – *see school* – *effective school.*

school ethos – *see school climate.*

school-focused in-service training – *see training.*

School Governing Body (Board of Governors) – a board of representatives of the local community (parents, teachers including the headteacher, business people, local politicians) who have ultimate responsibility for the management of a school.

schooling – that part of a pupil's education which takes place in school.

school leader – a term used in Scandinavian countries for headteacher.

school leavers – the group of students finishing school at the end of their final year.

School Management Task Force (SMTF) – a part-time committee of six people established by the DFE from 1988–92 to advise on and promote educational management development in England and Wales.

school marketing – the process whereby schools identify the needs of their 'clients' or 'customers' (pupils and parents) and advertise their ability to meet those needs, for example, through published school prospectuses, open days, parents' evenings.

schoolmaster – a traditional name for a male school teacher, still employed, particularly in the private schools.

school meals supervisory assistant (SMSA) – a paid employee who supervises pupils during the school lunch hour when meals are served in school.

schoolmistress – a traditional term for a female teacher, now increasingly replaced by the gender-neutral term school teacher.

School of Education – a department within a higher education institution which conducts research and teaching in the field of education and is responsible for pre-service and in-service education.

school phobia/refusal – a psychological hatred of attending school experienced by a small number of children.

school premises – the buildings and grounds belonging to a school.

school prospectus – the brochure or booklet which outlines what the school has to offer to pupils and parents.

School Psychology Service – *see Educational Psychology Service.*

secondment – the temporary allocation of a teacher or lecturer to another institution away from his or her normal place of employment in order to improve professional knowledge and skills, for example, a secondment to an industrial organization to observe management practices.

Secretary of State for Education – the senior minister, an elected politician and member of the Cabinet, who is responsible for leading the Department for Education and its team of ministers, *see Minister of Education.*

Section 11 – the label of legislation by which the Home Office provides funding for the support in schools of children who speak English as a second language, *see teacher – Section 11.*

sector – in the educational system a large subdivision based on phase or level (primary, secondary, tertiary sectors) or on source of funding (state/public or private sectors).

selective education – a system of schooling in which children are selected for different types of schools on the basis of their performance on tests of aptitude and academic ability, *see school – grammar and secondary modern.*

self-actualization – the psychological state enjoyed by high performing people who have a sense of functioning at their full potential in most aspects of their life and work.

self-assessment/evaluation/review – the use of criteria by individuals or organizations to judge their own performance or value without the aid of outside agents.

self-developing school – *see school.*

self-development – the process of engaging in activities which will lead to self-improvement without depending on the help of outside agents.

self-fulfilling prophecy – the tendency of people to behave in line with the labels that others give them, for example, 'slow learners' or 'high fliers'.

self-image/concept – the way people see themselves, often subconsciously, which is thought strongly to influence their self-esteem and consequent behaviour.

self-managing school – *see school.*

self-monitoring – *see monitoring.*

self-motivation – *see motivation.*

semester – a division of an academic year usually into two parts of fifteen or more weeks, mainly used by universities in America, but increasingly in Britain.

seminar – the meeting of a group of students with a tutor to present and discuss a paper.

Senate – the governing body of a university, comprising senior academics and members of the community.

Senior Chief Inspector – *see inspector.*

senior lecturer – *see lecturer.*

Senior Management Team (SMT) – the top management team of teachers (not governors) in a school usually comprised of head-teacher, deputies and senior teachers.

setting – the grouping of pupils according to their ability in a subject for lessons in that subject.

shadowing – a staff development activity which involves following a colleague throughout the day in order to analyse and learn from her or his performance.

short course – *see course.*

site-based management – *see management – school-based management.*

skills – specific abilities or competencies which allow the proficient performance of tasks.

social change – *see change.*

social skills – the level of effectiveness demonstrated by an individual in a variety of social situations.

special education – the part of the education system which provides for people with special educational needs, both within mainstream schools and in specialist institutions.

special educational needs (SEN) – the term for a category of learners who need extra support in their formal education as a result of particular cognitive, emotional, behavioural or physical disabilities.

specialization – the concentration of provision into a narrower area of need for example, students seeking A-level qualifications specialize in three subjects in years 12 and 13.

special needs assistant (SNA) – a paid helper, usually in primary schools, allocated to a particular child who has been 'statemented' as needing special support to overcome learning difficulties.

split site school – *see school.*

staff – all the employees of an organization.

staff appraisal – *see appraisal.*

staff development – *see development.*

staff development days – days set aside in the school year when pupils do not attend school so that teachers can engage in professional development activities.

stakeholders – all those who have a vested interest or 'stake' in the success of an organization such as a school.

standardization – the process of producing a common standard to which all items conform for example, in the construction of tests or examinations to make them reliable.

standard national scale – the basic national pay spine for teachers with no additional incentive allowances.

standards – desired levels of quality or performance.

    standards of education – levels of achievement in learning which are expected to be attained as a result of formal instruction.

standard spending assessment (SSA) – the amount of central government funding per pupil allocated to each Local Education Authority according to a formula which varies from LEA to LEA.

statemented pupil – *see pupil.*

statementing – the process of assessing and classifying a pupil's special needs as a basis for providing additional resources to meet such needs.

statement of attainment – a description of what pupils should be able to do in order to achieve one of the eight levels of attainment into which subjects in the National Curriculum are divided.

status – the relative position of a person or product in a hierarchy of position or value.

    pupil/student status – the degree of esteem in which pupils are held.

    school status – the reputation and standing of a school in the eyes of the community.

    teacher status – the regard in which teachers are held in a country or community.

statutory instruments – documents of three types – regulations, rules and orders – which set out clarifications to and modifications of legislation contained in Acts of Parliament.

statutory orders – directives from a government department which set out in more detail the intentions of an Act of Parliament, for example, the orders relating to the various National Curriculum subjects which followed the 1988 Education Reform Act.

steering committee/group – *see committee.*

stereotype – an oversimple or distorted representation and labelling of a complex person, role or situation.

strategic planning – *see planning.*

strategy – broad approaches to making decisions that influence an organization's long-run performance.

win/lose strategy – when only one party in a conflict emerges as winner.

win/win strategy – where both parties in a conflict emerge with a sense of gain or dignity.

zero sum game – *see win/lose strategy above.*

streaming – organizing classes in schools on the basis of general ability so that in most subjects an assumed homogeneity of ability makes whole class teaching or didactic presentation feasible.

stress management – *see management.*

student – a person engaged in systematic learning in a particular field usually in secondary school or beyond.

student council – a representative body of students in an educational institution who are consulted on matters relating to student welfare and policy.

study leave – a period of leave, usually with pay, made available usually to lecturers in further or higher education to attend professional or academic courses, or complete a project.

subject – the basic courses of study into which a curriculum is divided derived from traditional academic disciplines for example, maths, history or newer fields of study for example, design and technology.

> **core subjects** – the three compulsory subjects in the National Curriculum – maths, English, science.

> **foundation subjects** – the seven subjects, in addition to core subjects, required to be taught as part of the National Curriculum – modern language, history, geography, technology, music, art, physical education.

> **subject adviser** – *see adviser.*

> **subject option** – one of several subjects which can be chosen by a student in addition to the compulsory core and foundation subjects.

subordinates – people who are subjected to the authority of their bosses or superordinates.

success criteria – descriptions of standards with which to measure whether an objective has been reached, *see performance indicators.*

summative evaluation – *see evaluation.*

superordinates – people in formal hierarchic organizations or line management structures who exercise authority over their subordinates.

supervision – the monitoring of the performance of a person by a supervisor.

clinical supervision – an American term for the practice of lesson observation by school principals (headteachers) in order to assess and develop the classroom skills of teachers.

dissertation supervision – the guidance by a tutor of a major research project conducted by a student in higher education as part of a degree course.

supervisor – a person who is responsible for monitoring the performance of others.

supply cover/supply/supply teachers – teachers who are available to substitute when other teachers are absent from school.

support staff – *see teacher support staff.*

survey – to collect information or opinion systematically from a sample of a population as a basis for research or policy making.

> **parent survey** – sampling parents' opinions about a proposed change in school policy for example, about a proposed change in the length of the school day or school uniform.
>
> **survey population** – the entire group about which a sample of opinion is taken.
>
> **survey sample** – the percentage of a given population from whom information is obtained.

SWOT analysis – a survey of an organization's strengths, weaknesses, opportunities and threats, both internal and external, in preparation for the production of a business or development plan.

syllabus – an outline in summary of the aims and contents of a course offered by an educational institution.

synergy – a term from physics used to mean when the results of the group interaction of individuals exceed what they could achieve through their separate efforts, that is, the whole is greater than the sum of the parts.

systematic – proceeding in a thought out, orderly, step-by-step manner.

T

targets – *see 'objectives'.*

task – a discrete amount of work which has to be achieved in order to obtain a result.

task force – a temporary group of professionals created to undertake a specific project or to advise the government for example, School Management Task Force which advised the DFE from 1988 to 1992.

teacher – a person who systematically helps people to learn, usually in an educational institution.

advisory teacher – an experienced teacher who is appointed or seconded for a short term by a Local Education Authority to advise school staff and provide in-service training and on-the-job support to teachers, often in the classroom.

articled teacher – graduates who take a two year, school-based PGCE course with support from an approved teacher training institution.

at risk/failing teacher – a teacher whose performance is sufficiently below normal levels of competence to warrant special intervention in order to remedy the situation.

licensed teacher – a not yet fully qualified teacher on a two year on-the-job programme of induction into the profession who is 'on licence' to teach full time.

newly-appointed teacher – a teacher who has just started to work in a new post.

newly-qualified teacher (NQT) – a new graduate from a pre-service teacher training course in the first year of employment as a teacher.

peripatetic teacher – a teacher, commonly of music, who moves between and teaches in several different schools each week.

probationary teacher – a teacher who has not yet completed the first full year of teaching and is not regarded as fully qualified, a status which was abolished in 1986.

Section 11 teacher – a teacher funded by the Home Office to support learning with children whose mother tongue is not English.

senior teacher – a title given to the most highly paid teachers who are one rank below deputy head but who are often in the senior management team of a school.

supply teacher – *see supply cover.*

support teacher – an additional teacher who gives support in the classroom to pupils with special needs such as second language or learning difficulties.

Teacher Centre – an institution usually provided by a local education authority where teachers at all levels can engage in in-service education and training, curriculum development, borrow teaching resources or meet for social purposes.

teacher education days – *see staff development days.*

teachers' aide – a person without teaching qualifications who is paid to act as a helper, usually in primary school classrooms.

teacher support staff – depending on the type of school, support staff for teachers consists of secretaries, classroom help, nursery nurses, laboratory technicians, whose purpose is to carry out non-professional work required in the classroom and school.

Teacher Training Agency (TTA) – a quango established by the government in 1994 to fund and oversee the provision of teacher education.

teaching force – the general term for all the teachers in a country.

teaching load – the number of lessons per week which individual teachers teach.

team – a group of people who collaborate for a common purpose.

    team building – a conscious effort to develop effective work groups throughout an organization.

    team teaching – the organization of classes so that several teachers can collaborate in teaching a large group of students flexibly, sharing the tasks of preparation and presentation.

    teamwork – the process in which a group of people collaborate in order to achieve a common purpose.

technical education – education designed to equip students with particular skills to prepare them for employment in a technical field for example, engineering, vehicle maintenance.

technician – an employee on the ancillary staff of an education institution who provides technical support in audio-visual resource and computer centres, laboratories and workshops.

technofix – a pejorative term which implies an excessive faith in technology as the solution to problems, overlooking the need for political, cultural or educational solutions.

tenure – the guarantee of permanent employment.

term – one of three sessions usually named Autumn, Spring and Summer Terms, each from ten to fourteen weeks long, into which the educational year is divided.

terms of reference – guidelines and criteria provided for drawing up project bids or contracts.

test – a formal evaluation of ability, achievement of quality.

criterion-referenced test – a test which measures performance against descriptive criteria, standards or levels of performance, thereby assessing what a person can do rather than comparing performance between different candidates.

norm-referenced test – a test designed to measure the performance of candidates in order to place them in an order of merit and to compare performance of the whole group with the norm or average performance.

theory – systematically organized assumptions and principles which seek to explain the nature of, or predict behaviour in, a particular field of knowledge or practice for example, management theory, contingency theory of leadership.

thesis – a written report on research conducted in pursuit of a masters or doctors degree, *see dissertation*.

three Rs – a tag phrase for the subjects of reading, writing and arithmetic.

three-tier system – the organization of schools in a minority of LEAs into three levels (first, middle and senior schools) rather than the more common primary and secondary levels.

time allocation – the amount of time provided for a particular activity.

time management – *see management*.

timetable – a schedule of activities set out chronologically for example, a school timetable which sets out the pattern of lessons for each class and subject.

top-down approach – *see approach*.

total quality management (TQM) – *see management*.

trade union – *see union*.

trainer – an expert who provides learning activities to develop people's skills.

training – structured learning activities designed to prepare people to carry out particular tasks or roles skilfully.

assertiveness training – systematic learning experiences provided by a trainer and designed to help managers and others claim their rights and make demands in a firm, reasonable, non-aggressive manner.

close-to-the-job training – activities or courses held in school about school performance but not involving direct observation and feedback.

experiential training – training by giving the trainee much opportunity to learn through experience; learning by doing.

off-site/off-the-job training – training activities conducted away from the workplace in places such as teachers' centres or higher education institutions.

on-site training – training conducted in the workplace.

outdoor training – leadership training conducted in the countryside in which managers are challenged to complete challenging tasks in teams to develop their initiative and self-confidence, or to develop their ability to cope with stress.

pre-service teacher training – the formal course and school-based teaching practice followed by teachers to prepare them to become qualified teachers.

school-based management training – management training of teachers carried out in their own school.

school-centred management training – management training of teachers from the same school, which may not be school-based, which focuses on the unique needs of that school.

school-focused in-service training – *see school-centred management training.*

vocational training – training for a specific job rather than general skills training.

Training and Enterprise Council (TEC) – a regional quango which funds local training initiatives in a variety of occupational sectors, including education.

Training Enterprise and Education Directorate (TEED) – the branch of the Department of Employment, originally called the Manpower Services Commission, which has responsibility for employment training in many occupational sectors and has become increasingly involved in funding educational initiatives in recent years.

transitional arrangements – the procedures, now completed, for changing over from LEA to school-based budgeting required by LMS legislation.

transparency – the policy within an organization of making the budgets and decision-making processes open to scrutiny, *see management – open management.*

tutor – a provider of individual advice, guidance and supervision for individual or small groups of students.

admissions tutor – the tutor who deals with applications and interviews for new students in further and higher education institutions.

home tutor – a teacher who provides tuition in a pupil's own home, *see home tuition.*

link tutor – a lecturer in one institution who is responsible for co-ordinating activities with another institution for example, between a teacher training college and primary or secondary schools.

programme tutor – a person, usually in further or higher education, who co-ordinates a whole programme involving several courses for example, M.Ed. programme tutor in a School of Education.

two-tier local authorities – local government authorities organized below national government into two hierarchic levels with county or metropolitan authorities (first tier) subdivided into subordinate district authorities (second tier).

two-way communication – *see communication.*

U

unconscious competence – *see competence.*

unconscious motivation – *see motivation.*

underachiever – a person who appears to be performing well below capacity, thereby presenting a management or teaching problem.

underperformer – *see underachiever.*

unions – more correctly trades unions, organizations of workers which have been formed to protect their interests, including in the educational service, NUT, UNISON, *see professional associations.*

unit – an individual component of a larger organization.

partially hearing unit – a classroom in a secondary school which is specially provided for teaching children with hearing difficulties.

remedial unit – a special unit in some schools where children with special educational needs receive specialist help and support.

unitary authority – a local government authority at district level being the only local administrative unit below the level of national government, *see two-tier local authorities.*

university – a higher education institution which is self-validating, conducts academic research and teaching usually to bachelor, masters and doctoral degree levels.

civic universities – universities such as Bristol, Manchester and Sheffield founded, often initially as university colleges, in provincial cities in the second half of the nineteenth century.

collegiate university – a university such as Cambridge, Durham and Oxford in which constituent colleges have a high degree of autonomy over endowments, student selection, property and staff appointments.

federal university – a university such as London in which colleges retain control over their internal affairs but a Senate approves policies and appointments.

Universities Funding Council (UFC) – the short-lived advisory body to the government on university funding created by the 1988 Education Reform Act and replaced by the HEFCE in 1992.

university college – a college which cannot award its own degrees but is affiliated with a federal or collegiate university.

university department of education (UDE) – *see School of Education*.

University Grants Committee (UGC) – an advisory body to the government on university funding, established in 1919 and replaced by the UFC following the 1988 Education Reform Act.

university leavers – students who finish their university programme and depart to start their careers.

university premises – the buildings and grounds owned or leased by a university.

university prospectus – the marketing brochure which describes for potential students the programmes, facilities and opportunities available in a university.

upgrading – the process of improving one's qualifications.

V

vacation – the gaps between university terms at Christmas, Easter and in the Summer.

validation – the inspection of degree courses in a college of education which cannot award its own degrees by a university or other accrediting body which can, in order to guarantee the standard of the award, *see accreditation*.

value-added – the comparison of output with input data to measure increases in productivity over a given period as in attempts to compare the test or examination results of the same pupils over time.

Vice-chancellor – the chief executive or director of a university.

village college – *see college.*

virement – moving funds from one part of a budget to another.

vision – the imagined successful future for an organization or individual arising from basic values or philosophy, to which one links goals and plans.

vocational education – education designed to prepare students for the world of work for example, hairdressing or word processing courses.

voluntary-aided school – *see school.*

voluntary-controlled school – *see school.*

voluntary time – time spent on professional activities which is at the discretion of the individual teacher.

W

warden –

a) the principal of a community or village college.

b) a Teacher Centre Leader.

c) the person in charge of a hall of residence in a university or college.

welfare assistant – a person who is not a qualified teacher but is employed by a Local Education Authority to help teachers with children who have special educational needs.

White (policy or Command) Paper – a paper issued by the command of a head of a government department such as the Secretary of State for Education, to bring reports or proposals for legislation before the House of Commons and to invite comments from other interested parties.

win/lose strategy – *see strategy.*

win/win strategy – *see strategy.*

work experience – the provision of opportunity for students to have a short, direct experience of the world of work by being attached to a specific enterprise as part of a course of study.

working conditions – the actual physical and social setting in a workplace.

working party – a temporary group of employees within an organization who are invited to investigate and advise on policy issues or produce solutions to specific problems.

workload – the amount of work a person must accomplish in a given time.

Y

year/year group – a specific age group within a school, for example, Year 7 consists of all 11–12-year-old pupils.

year head – *see head of year.*

Youth Service – staff and facilities, often in schools in the evenings, provided by the Local Education Authority to give young people additional social, recreational and cultural experience.

Z

zero-base budgeting – *see budgeting.*

zero sum game – *see strategy.*

2

TOPIC ESSAYS

ACCOUNTABILITY

Until the mid-1970s the word 'accountability' was rarely, if ever, heard in schools. Certainly there is little trace of it in the education management literature in this era. Headteachers would doubtless consider the school staff as accountable to them, but there would be no means of evaluating the effectiveness of loosely defined expectations, other than through their professional experience. Job descriptions were used for the purpose of advertising vacancies and were rarely used other than for a comparison of applications with the requirements of the post. At a more senior level, job descriptions were likely to include tasks expected of the incumbent and said little about roles.

If asked about their accountability, headteachers would doubt-less cite the school managers or governors, and the LEA. The powers of the former were then largely formal (*see School Governors*) and many LEAs held that the appointment of a good school leader was a guarantee of effectiveness. There was accountability through HMI inspections but, save in exceptional circumstances, remedying discovered shortcomings was largely an internal matter for the school, with support from the LEA if needed.

Four significant developments in the 1980s led to a marked re-consideration of accountability within and without the school:

- First, there was the introduction of government funded initia-tives such as the Technical and Vocational Education Initiative

(TVEI) which required that schools account for the funding provided by meeting success criteria.

- Secondly, there was a growing understanding among senior managers in schools that there was a climate of public demand that schools should become more aware of the external environment. There began the consideration of such questions as accountability to whom – parents, pupils, ratepayers and taxpayers, governors, the education committee, the LEA, the community at large? The question 'who is the client?' is still a vexed one within the profession.
- Thirdly, the negotiations and discussion in the mid-1980s on appraisal led to an increasing awareness in schools that teaching standards and accountability were closely related.
- Fourthly, and most powerfully, the devolution implicit in local financial management (LFM) and local management of schools (LMS) demands high levels of accountability.

Accountability requires clear answers to the questions: who is accountable, for what and to whom? It also raises the question: who determines what is acceptable as evidence of accountability? The criteria may be established by central government, but, even when this is the case, it still remains for the school to make them effective in the light of its own circumstances.

ASSESSMENT

School pupils have always been assessed, often by primitive and unreliable means. There have been teachers who claimed that to give high grades would lead their pupils to become complacent. There were others who argued that, however substandard the quality of the work, the effort was worthy of encouragement, and gave an assessment that bore no relation to the work of more able pupils in a parallel class. Yet others, teaching subjects with a high level of creativity, have claimed that, so subjective is the concept of 'good', there is no justification for giving any assessment at all. It is important from the outset to separate the concept of assessment from that of providing incentives, by whatever means.

There are two main types of assessment, norm-referenced and criterion-referenced. The former compares the performance of a pupil with that of others, but gives no indication of what has been achieved. The latter provides indicators to more fundamental

questions: about the competence of the teaching; whether there is
need for remedial attention for a particular pupil; whether the
standards of individuals or groups of pupils are being maintained;
if standards are declining or improving; what general assumptions
might be made about the possible reasons.

The Dunning Committee (1977) argued that assessment 'should
make a positive contribution to the teaching and learning process'.
Assessment therefore has a dual role: to be both formative and
diagnostic. If it is not a continuous process, one where pupil outcomes are routinely recorded and assessed and the implications of
teacher inputs regularly considered, then it will not fulfil either
role.

Summative assessment poses particular problems. The domains
tend to be large. The National Curriculum classifies English into
three domains: speaking and listening, reading, and writing. Each
of these can be broken down into a number of sub-domains: the
purpose of writing, for example, may be to convey information, to
argue a case, to express feelings and up to half a dozen more
aspects of the skill. It is relatively easy to generalize about a pupil's
standards in a given skill, but far more difficult to assess the components of that skill. Here performance indicators are valuable in
enabling teachers to have common ground for their assessment,
without excessive direction.

Nor should self-assessment be overlooked as an element in the
diagnostic and formative process, even from a very early age. Peer-
assessment is particularly valuable in group-work learning
situations.

COMMUNITY EDUCATION

Community education grew out of nineteenth century
philanthropy, as the need both for promoting adult literacy and for
providing useful activities for working class boys and girls became
increasingly recognized. There was no state responsibility for
youth work and adult education until well into the next century.
The idea that both might be integrated into a purpose-built school
began when the concept of the Village College was realized in
Cambridgeshire in the 1930s.

Although the war halted the extension of this development, it
was to provide the opportunity for Local Education Authorities

(LEAs) to consider the economies arising from provision in their new schools for the growing recreational and educational needs of young people and adults. This happened initially mainly in the New Towns – conceived to limit the further expansion of existing conurbations – and in semi-rural areas, both of which would otherwise have been seriously deprived of social amenities. These institutions were called community schools and in some places community colleges. Later they were to develop also in urban areas.

The headteacher, often called warden or principal, has overall responsibility for all the activities in the community school. The staff usually includes a part- or full-time community tutor, and in some community colleges the post is that of community vice-principal. Responsibility for devising and running the programme rests with the professional staff, but budgeting and policy are decided by the community council on which the users have elected representatives. In most community schools and colleges some governors serve on the council and some council members on the governing body.

There are fees for educational and recreational classes, since most tutors require to be paid. Often these tutors are full-time teachers in the day school. Clubs may be organized by community members themselves, with the membership fee inclusive of a contribution to the maintenance of the premises and its facilities. Outside organizations hire parts of the premises, in particular the sports facilities, or the theatre for plays and concerts.

Many countries are developing, in ways which suit their own conditions, what is increasingly known as life-long education. In Latin America, for example, the need for basic education is met by the 'each one teach one' principle behind Paulo Freire's teaching. In the USA the long tradition of the community school programme began in the state of Michigan in the early 1930s by an alliance between C. S. Mott, a philanthropist, and Frank Manley, then a young physical education teacher. Such programmes are now to be found in every state.

EDUCATIONAL PLANNING

The term mission statement is widely used in North America and has spread to other English-speaking countries, including the

United Kingdom. It is a philosophical statement of the purpose of the institution, and is as appropriate to schools as to businesses or government departments. It must be concise and well thought out. The following example is taken from an English primary school, where the headteacher and staff drafted the mission statement for governors' approval.

> The school is committed to preserving and expanding its aims for a caring environment where all are enabled to develop and fulfil their whole potential.

There is no attempt in the mission statement to describe how its intentions will be achieved. The mission statement must therefore be translated into:

Aims / goals

Aims – sometimes called purposes – are general statements of the direction in which an organization desires to move. Goals are similarly defined, except that there is more emphasis on desired results. There are two elements to the above mission statement that will be translated into a series of aims or goals. To create a 'caring environment', for example, requires that the staff have clearly defined and agreed policies on how pupils in the school will be treated; on the school's relationship with parents; and on the relationship with the community within which the school is sited. To achieve each aim or goal, the school must devise a series of:

Objectives

These specify how aims or goals will be realized. They will be stated in clearly defined terms so that progress can be identified, in some cases even measured, and shortcomings examined. No school can deal with the totality of its aims and objectives at the same time. It is necessary therefore to prioritize. This is done through:

The school development plan

A rolling programme is set up of what the school intends to do over a period of time. Most schools find a three-year development plan a suitable format. The first year of the plan becomes a firm commitment of intent for that year. The second and third years are open to modification in the light of the experience of the first year, usually at or near its conclusion. External factors may also promote changes. At the end of each year, the plan is extended into a further year so that there is always a three-year perspective.

See also: Managing Change.

INSPECTION (1)– Her Majesty's Inspectorate

For at least three post-war decades schools were regarded as institutions staffed by trained teachers whose professionalism was considered to be sufficient guarantee of the quality of their work. Schools were, in other words, largely self-accountable. The role of Local Education Authority (LEA) advisers was partly to have a broad oversight of the quality of schooling in the LEA, but more particularly to respond to requests from schools for help and advice. Advisers promoted LEA-based in-service training and had a particular responsibility for the probationary period of newly qualified teachers. They adopted the role of inspector reluctantly, usually only when a school appeared to be failing.

Her Majesty's Inspectorate (HMI) was responsible for school inspection and reported direct to the Secretary of State for Education. There were three types of inspection: 'dipstick', where a random sample of schools provided a general overview of educational standards; selective, in which a range of schools were visited in the course of research for a publication commissioned by the Secretary of State or felt by HMI to be of value to improvement in professional practice and standards; and, relatively rarely, inspection of a school regarded as in imminent danger of breakdown. Inspectors were appointed from the ranks of experienced and successful teachers.

A full inspection might be viewed with alarm by the staff of a school, since it could last a week, required an immense amount of preparatory documentation and entailed the presence at the back of the classroom of an inspector taking copious notes. Yet the HMI visitation was rarely as threatening as had been anticipated. Subject specialist HMIs spoke to class teachers individually or, in secondary schools, often in departmental meetings, about what was good and what improvements might be made. After the team meeting at the end of the inspection the team leader gave the headteacher a verbal report, during which any misunderstandings or factual errors might be corrected. A verbal report was given to governors and a written report published, often considerably later. Usually the two latter reports aimed to make positive recommendations rather than adverse criticisms, relying on the school management to respond to weaknesses with the help of the LEA.

All this was to change with the virtual dissolution of HMI and its replacement by the Office for Standards in Education (OFSTED). *See Inspection (2).*

INSPECTION (2)
– Office for Standards in Education

The Office for Standards in Education (OFSTED) was created in 1992 when Her Majesty's Inspectorate (HMI) was drastically reduced in numbers and reorganized. OFSTED brought about a new and rigorous type of inspection applicable to all state schools. It is directed by Her Majesty's Chief Inspector (HMCI) and is completely independent of the Department for Education and Employment (DFEE) and the government.

HMCI's first task was to establish a register of trained inspectors as team leaders. All members of an inspectorial team – registered inspectors, team members and lay inspectors – have had to pass an approved course of training. Lay inspectors, one in each team, are intended to provide a common-sense view from those not professionally involved in education: those with financial or business expertise, for example.

For each planned inspection at least two tenders must be invited from registered inspectors able to draw together a suitable team for the type of school to be inspected. This condition is increasingly not being met, and the intention that every school will be inspected every four years seems most unlikely to be achieved. If inspection were to concentrate largely on failing schools, a possibility if the number of trained and available inspectors is insufficient, then the expected overview of educational standards is likely to become distorted.

OFSTED provides for every school a framework of inspection covering the principles of what will be looked for: the quality of education provided; the educational standards achieved; the efficient management of financial resources; the spiritual, moral, social and cultural development of pupils. There is concern among schools and LEAs that insufficient attention may be paid to local circumstances: the very recent appointment to a failing school of a new headteacher, for example; disruptive changes brought about by the departure of key members of staff; financial cutbacks; the socio-economic conditions in the neighbourhood.

HMCI reports annually to the Secretary of State for Education on the findings of inspection reports. The complete report on an individual school is available to anyone requesting it; all parents receive a summary. School governors have a duty to prepare an action plan setting out what they propose to do in response to the report and over what period of time. This goes to HMCI and is available to parents and other interested parties.

LEADERSHIP

The use in England and Wales of the term 'headteacher' instead of 'principal' as used in Scotland and in most other countries derives from the fact that traditionally, the headteacher has ascended the ladder within the profession from classroom to study. For many years, even in the post-war period as schools grew bigger and organizationally more complex, headteachers argued that it was important that they demonstrated their leadership by taking on some teaching commitment. In small primary schools, of course, there was never any choice: the headteacher is still today a full-time teacher, possibly relieved for half a day for administration.

School leadership has become increasingly complex and more demanding. During the 1980s there were repeated exhortations such as that from an HMI report that 'leadership of the head-teacher determines the quality of education throughout the school'. Yet, in spite of considerable research in industry and education at this time, the style of school leadership remained idio-syncratic. One study of primary headteachers identified three styles:

- the passive: the headteacher who gives staff more freedom than they desire;
- the bourbon: the headteacher who maintains a social distance in an attempt to assert authority over staff;
- the positive: the headteacher who sets high professional standards, as well as consulting with staff.

These styles are as relevant to secondary headteachers as to primary. Indeed, as the concept of leadership has moved steadily from hierarchical to collegial, so the adoption by all staff with leadership responsibilities of the third model is of crucial import-ance to the ability of the school to cope with the demands of rapid change and accountability. Furthermore, there are two key and complementary aspects of leadership which can determine how well a school is managed: transforming leadership, whereby all staff interact to improve motivation; and transactional leadership which reflects the various processes of negotiation which take place in the school organization.

In many countries, the United States for example, promotion to headship is conditional on advanced training and qualification. In the UK, despite some improvement in the past ten years or so, there is still too little training for school leadership at all levels. In well managed schools training will take place within the institu-tion, formally and by example. In failing schools the role model presented by the headteacher may stifle leadership initiative and lower school effectiveness.

LEGISLATION

The way laws are made in the British Parliament is important to an understanding of how educational changes come about. Parlia-ment has two chambers: the House of Commons and the House of Lords. The first stage is the drafting of a Commons Bill by special-ist lawyers employed by Parliament and knowledgeable about the need to comply with the House rules. A draft version will usually be seen by government ministers and, if the wording is satisfactory, the Bill begins its stages through the Commons.

The First Reading is merely formal: the Clerk of the House reads its title and the names of its presenters. The Bill is then printed in full for all Members to see and a date named for the Second Reading, when the Commons discusses the Bill in prin-ciple. Because it would be cumbersome for over 600 Members to propose amendments, the Bill is passed to a Standing Committee which examines it clause by clause. This committee may amend the Bill but cannot reject it.

The House next debates it in its amended form and may require that it is further amended. Finally, it is given a Third Reading, when it is voted upon. If the vote is favourable, it goes to the House of Lords, which may also propose amendments or vote the Bill down. Amendments will be considered by the Commons and the Bill is now ready to receive the Royal Assent and become an Act of Parliament. If the House of Lords has voted down the Bill, the Commons may simply present it again, with or without amendments: the House of Lords has no powers to reject it a second time.

An Act may contain delegated legislation, whereby a Minister is empowered to make rules and regulations later to give it effect. The complexity of an Act may make it impossible to cover in advance every contingency. This power has sometimes been controversial: the 1986 Education (No. 2) Act contained over 300 instances where decisions were left to Ministers. Those applicable to teacher appraisal were not finalized until 1989, during which time different Ministers announced a succession of variant draft regulations.

The term Green Paper is used when the government seeks the opinion of interested parties while official policy is at a formative stage. A White Paper, on the other hand, offers interested parties the chance to study the government's intention in advance of a proposed enactment and to express opinions.

LOCAL EDUCATION AUTHORITY (LEA)

In England and Wales every 'first-tier' authority controls policy and spending through its committees. First-tier authorities are counties and, in large conurbations, metropolitan boroughs. In 1996 – in Wales 1997 – some counties will be subdivided into districts with first-tier powers.

From the elected councillors on these first-tier authorities a given number will be chosen to serve on the education committee, usually in proportion to the strength of the political parties on the council. It is usual for there to be in addition co-opted members, some representing teacher interests.

The Local Education Authority is a term that describes both the education committee and its subcommittees and the paid officers to whom day-to-day decisions are delegated. The officers are led by the Chief Education Officer, in some authorities called the Director of Education. There will be several deputy directors and assistant directors, each with specific roles, and a number of officers with various responsibilities. There is also a Chief Inspector – formerly more usually called Chief Adviser – who heads a team of inspectors/advisers responsible for supporting schools and maintaining standards. It is usual for advisers to have two roles: a phase (primary or secondary, for example) and/or curriculum subject specialism; and responsibility for liaison with a group of the LEA schools, usually on a geographical basis. In LEAs with large ethnic minorities there will be a multicultural adviser.

The powers of the LEA have been declining rapidly since the 1980s. First, the proportion of central government's contribution to the cost of education has declined year by year. This left councils with the task of raising more money from local rates, now known as the community charge; but the amount that councils may raise is controlled by government 'capping' with severe penalties for overspending. Secondly, with the introduction of local financial management in schools LEAs had to delegate the funding of much of their work to the schools and therefore to 'market forces'.

There are still some specialized services maintained by the LEA from retained funds: the Education Psychological Service is one such. The Education Welfare Service is available to schools for cases of long-term truancy that may need to be brought before the Juvenile Court; and many LEAs provide residential care for the support and education of pregnant girls and child-mothers still of compulsory school age.

LOCAL FINANCIAL MANAGEMENT

The delegation in the 1988 Education Reform Act (ERA) of responsibility for the local management of schools (LMS) included legislation which gave school governors of all secondary schools and large primary schools – later extended to all primary schools – the management of their own budgets. Local Education Authorities had to delegate at least 85 per cent of their budget to schools. Schools, the DES argued, were now free to take expenditure decisions which matched their own priorities, and allowed to benefit from any efficiency savings.

This was not entirely an innovation. Pilot schemes had been running in a number of LEAs since 1981, but with significant variations in the amount of delegated responsibility. Their experience was undoubtedly of some value when Local Financial

Management (LFM) was introduced, but the lead-in time did not allow for adequate preparation. This ignored the four criteria for the successful implementation of the scheme detailed by the Chartered Institute of Public Finance and Accountability (CIPFA) that the successful implementation of the scheme depended on good management training of headteachers and governors; sound planning; good communication; and positive attitudes.

The concept that every school would need to provide for the detailed monitoring and control of revenue expenditure, whether delegated to other staff or not, alarmed those headteachers without budgetary skills and particularly in those schools lacking ancillary staff experienced in financial management (*see Staffing the School (2)*). Few were then aware – and some are still unaware – of the two main approaches to budgeting: incremental budgeting and zero-base budgeting (ZBB). The former is basically a roll forward, with new figures and slight adjustments, of the previous year's budget: inefficiency and misuse of resources will be perpetuated. The latter, developed mainly in the USA, requires spending departments to justify their proposed budget for both existing and new activities, and to evaluate the benefits to the school of each. This requires that the headteacher or the senior management team aggregates all proposed activities and produces an 'order of merit' with a cut-off point when the budget limits have been reached.

All budgeting requires that budget holders act with scrupulous concern for the school as a whole. A department may be tempted to overbid in order to anticipate the likelihood of cuts. The finance subcommittee of the school governors is the final arbiter of allocations, but for detail is dependent on the planning by the school staff.

MANAGING CHANGE

In the first half of the twentieth century, change in schools was minimal. Indeed, with staff changes rare and curriculum changes rarer still, the timetable for one year could be presented virtually unchanged for the next. The post-war need for new schools to remedy war damage and to provide for the rapidly growing child population enabled LEAs to introduce open-plan primary schools and to introduce comprehensive education at secondary level. In the present decade educational change appears to be accelerating rapidly in all countries.

Management by objectives (MBO)

This process, widely used in industry and commerce, was first used in schools in the early 1970s. Its four steps should be regarded as cyclic rather than sequential:

- Analyse the present situation (Where are we now?).
- Identify aims and objectives and prioritize them (Where are we going?).
- Decide on all the possible means of achieving them and establish criteria to decide the best means, having in mind available resources (How do we intend to get there?).
- Assess the extent to which the aims and objectives are being fulfilled (How do we know when we have got there?).

Internal change and externally imposed change

Internal change is easier to control, since a school may analyse its present situation and decide that the time is not appropriate for change, or that resources are not available. Change imposed by new legislation is now commonplace, and demands a response whether the school is ready for it or not. This is one of the main causes of stress in schools today.

Monitoring and evaluating

The difference between these two terms is that monitoring takes place throughout the change process, and evaluation at its conclusion. However, the term formative evaluation is also used, implying that evaluation takes place during the process to effect improvement.

A simple paradigm for implementing change once a decision to act has been taken is as follows:

Plan – Prepare – Perform – Evaluate
Monitor

Preparation must be monitored to ensure that the plan is being adhered to or to allow for any modification to it if the preparation indicates the need. Monitoring performance tests the plan and its preparation as well as ensuring that staff are adhering to both.

Evaluation, even in schools, requires an academic rigour, and should use questionnaires or face-to-face interviews or both. Help from the LEA or a university school of education can be valuable.

NATIONAL CURRICULUM

Introduced by the 1988 Education Reform Act (ERA), the National Curriculum legislated for every aspect of the curriculum in every state school in England and Wales.

For each subject there are four Key Stages: KS1 for pupils in Y1–2; KS2 for Y3–6, the normal ending of the primary phase; KS3 for Y7–9; and KS4 Y10–11, the age at which external examinations are normally taken. English, mathematics and science are core subjects; other subjects, seven in all, must be studied. For each subject and each key stage there is a programme of study, which is the basis for planning teaching and teacher assessment. In English, for example, the programme of study consists of speaking and listening, reading and writing, each divided into range – the learning context – key skills and language study. For each of these there is a precise description of what and how pupils should be taught.

There are attainment targets for each key stage, with a range from 1–10. There is overlap, but nevertheless there is an expectation that the great majority of pupils should be within levels 1–3 by the end of KS1, 2–5 by the end of KS2, and so on. There are precise level descriptors and teachers are expected to find the 'best fit' of two adjacent levels for each aspect of each subject through Standard Assessment Tasks (SATs) at the end of each key stage.

While there is obviously merit in co-ordinating the learning content for all children, teacher objections have centred on:

- the excessive specificity of content, which precluded them from following topics of general interest such as might arise from contemporary discoveries in science or events in history, for example;
- the amount of time taken up by the administration of SATs, depriving pupils of teaching time;
- the lack of recognition that the cumulative records kept by class and subject teachers enabled all but the least experienced or conscientious to identify the appropriate level at the end of a key stage without using SATs;

- the use of league tables to compare the performance of schools without regard for socio-economic and environmental factors affecting the school's intake.

There was initially widespread refusal among teachers to conduct the SATs. Modifications have since been introduced to the more extensive and constraining programmes of study, and the latest revision is now more acceptable to teachers. There is still professional concern about the publication of results in league tables.

PUBLIC EXAMINATIONS (1) – Academic

Unlike many European countries, the British curriculum was largely free of centralized control until recent times. The 1944 Education Act was prescriptive in one area only, that the curriculum must include Christian religious education, from which parents of other beliefs had the right to withdraw the participation of their children. The major controlling factor in what was taught was the syllabuses of the examinations externally set and marked by public examination boards: pre-war, the General and Higher School Certificates; post-war, the General Certificate of Education (GCE) at Ordinary (O) and Advanced (A) levels, taken customarily at sixteen and eighteen. There was a wide choice of subjects at both levels, the major determinants of which were ability, inclination, what the school could offer, and employer and higher education requirements.

The syllabus content was geared to the top 20 per cent of the academic ability range, traditionally those in the grammar schools. With the advent of comprehensive education, not only were there pupils of that ability in comprehensive schools, but increasingly, since there was no longer a set minimum of subjects required for certification, more and more pupils below that percentile were being entered for O-level. Nevertheless, competent pupils were being excluded from certification by the academic nature of the syllabuses. Schools increasingly went elsewhere for certification, and the government commissioned the Beloe Report which recommended a new five-grade examination in which a Grade 1 pass was the equivalent of an O-level pass. The first examinations were in 1965.

One consequence of the new Certificate of Secondary Education (CSE) was a proliferation of regional examination boards, of subjects and of subject syllabuses, the last exacerbated by the fact that schools could choose between a Mode 1 examination under the Board's syllabus marked externally and a Mode 3 examination under an approved school-based syllabus marked internally and moderated externally. There was in most CSE examinations an element of coursework, extensive in some school-based syllabuses. This was especially so in those designed for lower ability pupils, accepted by the Board provided there was a restriction on the grades awarded.

Inevitably, profusion and confusion led to the amalgamation of the GCE and CSE under the title of the General Certificate of Secondary Education (GCSE) governed by five regional boards and with syllabuses common to all abilities. The first candidates sat this new examination in 1988.

See Public Examinations (2) for vocational education.

PUBLIC EXAMINATIONS (2) – Vocational

Before 1965, when the Certificate of Secondary Education (CSE) was initiated, schools wishing to present their pupils for examination other than for the General Certificate of Education (GCE) increasingly looked to bodies awarding vocational qualifications. The one most used was the Royal Society of Arts (RSA), which awarded a succession of certificates in Shorthand and Typing based on increasing accuracy and speed. Although there were other aspects of business skills examined by this board, these skills were the most popular in schools since employment opportunities for shorthand typists were good, and the certificates provided incentives for pupils who would otherwise have no qualification. There was not seen to be a parallel demand for boys and girls taking technical subjects, since woodwork, metalwork, technical drawing, and, latterly, technology were available through the CSE and GCE boards. Nevertheless, even though there were some linked courses between comprehensive schools and technical colleges where geographical proximity made this possible, there was no national concept of a continuing role for vocational education.

The National Council for Vocational Qualifications (NCVQ) was set up in 1986 to rationalize all vocational qualifications. The main criteria for these qualifications were that:

- the syllabuses should be framed in close consultation with the employers and should take account of the rapid developments in technology;
- there must be 'statements of competence' within the specification of the qualification;
- each qualification may be gained by full-time study, or by workplace experience coupled with self-study, often using Open College materials;
- qualification would be based on the aggregation of a number of discrete units;
- there would be a progression through five levels of qualification that range from competence in work skills (level 1), through competence that includes the ability to supervise others (level 3) and was broadly equivalent to A-level standard, to a vocationally-related postgraduate qualification (level 5).

The awarding organizations – the Royal Society of Arts (RSA), the Business and Technology Educational Council (BTEC) and the City and Guilds – introduced in 1992 the General National Vocational Qualifications (GNVQ), as a full-time course in Year 12 in schools or further education.

Vocational education in the UK has long been seen as a poor relative of academic education. Recent measures such as those described here are expected to raise the status and standards of training for employment.

QUALITY MANAGEMENT

Quality management is a term that has been used in industry for many years. Only recently has its application to education management been explored and understood; it is based on the concept that *the quality of pupils' learning is at the heart of effective management.* There can be no absolute definition of quality. Quality management is concerned with fitness of purpose: while the central purpose of a school, as encapsulated in its mission statement, will hold good, there will be external and internal forces that will determine changes in the aims and objectives and will modify the steps that need to be taken to achieve quality.

There are three concepts of quality management:

Quality Control (QC) takes place *after* the process. In education it happens most frequently through external inspection. Its value is that it enables the school to take steps to remedy shortcomings next time round; but its principal defects are that it removes responsibility from those involved and that it implies a top-down model of management.

Quality Assurance (QA) takes place *before and during* the process. It aims to prevent failure by setting in advance clear standards of performance in the planning of which all those responsible for the process are involved. Its principal defect is that it is easy for management to become self-satisfied and carry the same standards forward year by year without reconsidering them, simply because they have been successful in the past.

Total Quality Management (TQM) takes place *before, during and after* the process and throughout the school. Clear standards of performance are set through unambiguous written statements of expectation, and both the standards themselves and the processes are regularly reviewed and improved by all concerned. Since quality is the responsibility of everybody in the school, staff development is an essential feature of TQM. The most effective way of achieving quality is through teamwork.

Some schools have set up quality circles, teams of teachers that cut across the traditional hierarchies and subject barriers. These teams, under an elected or appointed chairperson, review ways of improving the quality of the school's provision and make recommendations to the school's senior management, of which each Quality Circle chairperson is a member. There is consequently total involvement of all staff in quality management. Items for the agenda of meetings may come from any team member or from the senior management.

RESTRUCTURING AND TRANSFORMATION

In the early 1990s there was a growing awareness that meeting the needs of effective schooling could be brought about only through radical managerial change. In the USA there was a rising tide of anxiety about the nation's ability to continue to compete in the global market. In Australia, New Zealand and Canada there were moves to transform the basic components of educational systems through, for example, site-based management. In England and Wales the 1988 Education Reform Act (ERA) brought about a major shift to on-site managerial control through local management of schools (LMS) but without providing the necessary time or the funding for the extensive retraining of school leaders.

In the countries of the former communist bloc, the extent and rate of national change in the curriculum required to adapt to a market economy is a key issue. Here, the main focus is on change in the management of schools, on new national curricula, and on the development of new styles of teaching and learning for their effective delivery. In Poland, for example, an extensive programme financed mainly by the European Union aims progressively to cascade managerial transformation – a term becoming increasingly preferred to restructuring – from the ministry down to the school level.

Study of effective business concerns revealed that success resulted from the encouragement of autonomy, the pruning of bureaucracy to its essentials, and the institution's acceptance of a corporate culture. This contrasts with the way most schools have in the past performed. Changes in the prevailing educational management structures through incremental reform is unlikely to achieve the desired result. Restructuring is holistic. It must focus on the two prime areas of a school's activity: that of effective teaching and learning, and that of school governance.

In the USA there is some doubt about the ability of individual schools to restructure. Consequently, there are a number of major projects such as Washington State's 'Schools for the 21st Century' for which funding of $US 30 million was provided for a five-year period for 33 schools operating locally developed projects in school restructuring. The project was supported, monitored and evaluated by a directorate and in 1993 became the Center for the Improvement of Student Learning with indefinite state support. In other countries, including England and Wales, restructuring is undoubtedly occurring, though there is currently little cohesion in the individual efforts of schools.

SCHOOL GOVERNORS

It was not until the 1902 Education Act – which established Local Education Authorities (LEAs) – that it was ruled that all primary schools should have managers and all secondary schools governors. What managers and governors were to do was not defined. Even the Model Articles produced following the 1944 Education

Act were imprecise: they gave governors and managers responsibility for the care of the school premises and a 'share' – undefined – in budgeting and staff appointments and 'the general direction of the conduct and curriculum' of the school.

The 1980 Act removed the distinction between managers and governors and provided for the election of representatives of parents and teachers. It also introduced rules about the conduct of governors' proceedings but said nothing about their functions. However, the 1986 Act brought about radical change, prescribing governors' functions in relation to the curriculum, finance, staffing and discipline. It also required governors to convene an annual parents' meeting.

It was, however, the Education Reform Act (ERA) of 1988 that brought about far more fundamental change, to local management of schools (LMS). Governors now had full powers to hire school staff, whereas previously they could only recommend that the LEA appoint their chosen candidate. Subject to safeguards of natural justice, governors can also dismiss staff. They have extensive powers over the public funds of the school through local financial management (LFM). Headteachers and governors are required to work together to ensure that pupils receive the best possible education through the optimum use of resources. Many governing bodies are now looking at cost-benefit analysis of the budget allocation, the detailed deployment of resources, monitoring the effectiveness of decisions, and the evaluation of the school's major activities of caring and learning.

One major problem that arose from the vast extension of governor responsibilities and the changed constitution of the governing bodies was the need for governor training. There are excellent publications and courses available, but parent governors in particular – and there are 100,000 of these – do not necessarily have the background or the time to benefit from them. Turnover has been considerable, even though parents and community members have welcomed involvement in the governance of schools.

SCHOOL IMPROVEMENT AND EFFECTIVENESS

By the beginning of the 1980s there was a developing awareness that much of the curriculum development of the previous decade was random, sometimes idiosyncratic and often inadequately evaluated. School effectiveness, an essential component of social and economic well-being, required wider and more precisely articulated concerns than merely the content of the curriculum. Research was beginning to demonstrate that certain crucial qualitative factors enhance student outcomes: emphasis on the teaching/learning process accompanied by a common approach by the school staff; management-led agreement on goals; a supportive learning environment which includes good home–school relationships and parental involvement; and high expectations of academic achievement and the growth of social competence.

There was agreement in Western countries that a wide-ranging, collaborative, international study was needed that would have as its overall aim the dissemination of good practice in enhancing quality in schools. In 1982 the International School Improvement Project (ISIP) began after eighteen months of intensive planning. Fourteen countries, forty institutions and over 150 individual participants were involved for the next four years. The diverse nature of the educational political and social systems of these countries encouraged a radical appraisal of what was universally needed to promote school improvement and effectiveness.

ISIP worked through six area groups and its methodology included field visits, transnational pilot schemes, in-depth seminars and consultation within and across the groups. Dissemination, other than through fifteen topic publications, was through national and regional conferences. In the interim there had been published in England and Wales two White Papers, *Teaching Quality* (1983) and *Better Schools* (1985), but unaccompanied by any indication of how government might promote school effectiveness. The international benefits of the ISIP collaboration have been continued through the inauguration of the Foundation for International Collaboration on School Improvement (FICSI), with its headquarters in The Netherlands.

Even the major findings of so extensive a study cannot be summarized here. It is clear, however, that the culture of the school, the interpersonal relationships and the nature and quality of learning experiences are all-important. Their development depends on the qualities of leadership that exist in the school and the contribution to its management of the staff as a whole.

SCHOOLING (1) – Primary

In the United Kingdom compulsory education is from 5–16 and is free in the state system. Pre-school education can be obtained in one of four ways: in pre-school playgroups, run by parents, some of whom are trained and many of whom are volunteers; in private kindergarten, where the emphasis is more on formal learning; in nursery classes attached to primary schools and run by qualified professional staff; or by admission of rising fives into the reception class of primary schools, where numbers permit. In general the emphasis is on social and experiential learning, though it may be more structured in the kindergarten. Playgroups and kindergarten are often only half-day, are not state-funded, and take place usually in church halls or community rooms; but wherever they are held they must comply with stringent health and safety regulations. The introduction of vouchers will give parents choice in pre-school education for four-year-olds and financial support. There are some day nurseries, with a mainly social function, providing all-day care for children in need.

Schooling is by age from Reception (aged five or rising five on entry) to Year 11 (aged sixteen), with Years 12 and 13 for post-compulsory education in school (*see Schooling (2)*). The primary school covers R-Y6, an age range very different from that in many European countries. Even that age range may be subdivided into infants (R–Y2) and juniors (Y3–6), particularly when the two schools together might be deemed too large. They are often on the same campus.

Some LEAs have established first schools either for R–Y3 or R–Y4, followed by middle schools for Y4–7 or Y5–8 respectively, as the first two stages of the three-tier system. While the idea of more restricted age bands was once attractive, both educationally and socially, increased mobility in recent years, mainly through changing work patterns, has led to many children moving to schools in these LEAs feeling disadvantaged, even 'demoted'. There is now (*see curriculum*) the added complication that Key Stages 1 and 2 coincide with the end of the normal Infants and Junior stages respectively.

State-funded primary schools are described as either maintained or voluntary controlled. The latter are church schools – Church of England or Roman Catholic – with some governors, usually including the parish priest, appointed by the church. Governors of church schools have to abide by the same regulations as for maintained schools, except that they have greater control over the denominational content of religious education.

SCHOOLING (2) – Secondary

There are three possible age ranges for secondary schools: Y7–11, the second stage of compulsory schooling; Y7–13, including also post-compulsory schooling; Y9–13 or Y10–13, depending on the age range of the middle schools in the three-tier system. The movement towards comprehensive education has ground to a halt, and there are still over 100 selective grammar schools, which take pupils from Y7 on the basis of academic abilities demonstrated in the primary school and, usually, performance at interview. There are, however, some schools with a long history which retain the word 'grammar' in their names even though they are comprehensive!

The educational literature still often describes Y12–13 as the Sixth Form, another relic of a bygone age. Once most comprehensive schools which now cover only Y7–11 had 'sixth forms'; but, as the post-compulsory curriculum grew increasingly wider, it became uneconomic of teacher usage to maintain courses and classes for those over sixteen. Today there need to be special considerations, geographical or social, for Y12–13 education for fewer than 150 pupils to continue in comprehensive schools. Y11 is a suitable break-point, since the GCSE examinations are taken at the end of that year.

The first open-access Sixth Form Colleges date from the early 1970s, and within twenty years there were over 100, ranging in size from 300 to 1500 students, providing post-compulsory education for a quarter of England's 'sixth form' population. There had been, following the 1944 Education Act, a massive expansion in further education through full-time, day- and block-release. Coincident with the first Sixth Form Colleges, in those areas where further education institutions had successfully developed academic and vocational provision, post-compulsory education was offered in what were now called tertiary colleges. In the early 1990s there were over 50 such colleges, the average size of which is twice that of the sixth form colleges.

By the 1992 Further and Higher Education Act sixth form and tertiary colleges were amalgamated under the title corporate colleges and financed from central government. Each is a free-standing, autonomous institution responsible for its own affairs and runs a budget of several million pounds. College governors have the status of company directors.

SCHOOLING (3) – GM and CTC

State secondary schools, like primary schools, may be maintained or voluntary aided, under the control of the LEA. However, there are a number of schools which have taken advantage of provisions under the 1988 Education Reform Act (ERA) to opt out of local control and become directly funded by central government. These are known as grant-maintained (GM) schools. Opting out is through a majority vote of the parents of the school at the time application for GM status is made to the Department for Education (DFE). There is often community concern that those entitled to vote include the parents of those pupils who will have left, but not those whose children will have joined the school by the time the application is granted.

The reasons for application are varied. It was believed, correctly, that schools would benefit financially: for example, by 1991 GM schools had received for building maintenance on average four times as much as LEA schools. There are over one million 'spare' school secondary places in the school system, and LEAs are constantly urged by government to close or merge schools to save money. Yet when an LEA publishes its plan for retrenchment, many schools affected apply for GM status. Grammar schools made up 35 per cent of the successful applications by 1991, many to avoid a change of status. There have been a mere handful of applications from schools other than secondary; and overall a substantial number of ballots have rejected application for GM status.

At the same time the government introduced the concept of the City Technology Colleges. The intention was that there would initially be twenty of these funded jointly by government and the private sector of the economy. In practice only three-quarters of that total was reached when the government realized that the partner contributions were well below expectations and government was bearing the brunt of the funding. It was announced that no more would be launched 'for the time being'. These schools are, as their title implies, intended to be high-tech magnet schools, with a differential curriculum and high quality resources to meet the needs of their specialized fields and to attract the most promising pupils in the locality keenly interested in science and technology, or, in one case, the arts. It is too early to evaluate this experiment in terms of the heavy and continuing financial input.

SCHOOLING (4) – Independent

The use of the phrase public schools for those which are outside the state system is a long-standing tradition, but one which is very misleading to those from other countries. The nature of these schools is best understood if they are referred to as independent schools, since they are independent of both the Local Education Authority and government control. Their constitution is laid down in statutes and regulations, in particular through the Public Schools Act of 1868, or, since more than three-quarters of them are registered charities, through trust deeds.

The most satisfactory definition of an independent school is that it is in membership of one of the associations that subscribes to the Independent Schools Information Service (ISIS). This organization acts as a co-ordinator for statistics and information of use to prospective parents in particular. There are three key associations within ISIS. The Incorporated Association of Preparatory Schools (IAPS) has a membership of 560 preparatory schools which, as the name implies, prepares its pupils for entry into the public schools, usually at age thirteen, through the Common Entrance examination. There are very few preparatory schools exclusively for girls, but an increasing number admit both sexes. Since there is no requirement to conform to the National Curriculum, the preparatory schools' curriculum can be geared to the needs of the independent schools.

Most of the public schools are single-sex, though an increasing number admit girls to the sixth form, and cater for both boarding and day pupils. The Headmasters' Conference (HMC) has a membership of 225 schools and there are strict criteria for membership. The Girls' School Association (GSA) represents 245 girls' independent schools. The governing body is the ultimate authority in an independent school, its constitution a matter for the individual school. Nevertheless, in most independent schools it plays a role far less demanding than in state schools. It appoints the headmaster and possibly the bursar, but thereafter the headteacher has the role of chief executive responsible for educational policy, pupil admission and staff employment. Headteachers are on annual contracts, but there is little likelihood of these not being renewed unless standards fall dramatically. The bursar reports direct to the governing body on the school's finances.

The Assisted Places Scheme was instituted some years ago to enable academically able children, whose parents could not otherwise afford the high fees, to attend public schools.

SPECIAL EDUCATIONAL NEEDS
(1) – Learning Difficulties

It is only since the early 1980s that, following the Warnock Report (1978), there came about a general realization that special education is 'education first and special second'. The purpose of education and the goals are the same; only the help needed is different. It is now widely recognized that children with special educational needs should be integrated wherever possible in mainstream schools, since disabled and non-disabled children benefit from close association. The Education Act (1981) introduced integrated education, reversing the previous trend of establishing special schools and special units in ordinary schools.

The special education curriculum is now seen as distinctive but not different from mainstream education. Teaching these children is largely an extension of the skills required for teaching the wide range of abilities within any classroom. The concept of special educational needs has now been extended from the 2 per cent that formerly had segregated education to the 20 per cent who at some time in their school careers require extra help. Ideally this is provided within the school budget: in primary schools through the use of general assistants (GAs), in secondary schools by a specialist teacher with no class commitment able to help individuals and small groups by occasional withdrawal from their normal class or to support class teachers within their classroom. Both modes give flexibility and maintain the principle of integration.

There are some pupils, the 2 per cent referred to above, whose special educational needs cannot be met without significant extra resources. This requires statementing under section 5 of the Education Act (1981), a lengthy, formal and costly process involving the assessments of teachers, medical staff and other relevant specialists. Parents have a right to receive copies of all reports and to be present at assessment sessions. They may also initiate statementing procedures.

If it is decided to issue a statement of special educational needs, this becomes a legal contract between parents and the authority, outlining the provision which the LEA will make to meet the pupil's needs. There must be regular assessment of progress. The main weakness of statementing is that it is a long-drawn-out process, often further delayed by bureaucracy, and a year or more may elapse before action is taken to provide the necessary educational support. There has recently been issued a Code of Practice for the guidance of schools and parents.

See Special Educational Needs (2) for physical disabilities.

SPECIAL EDUCATIONAL NEEDS
(2) – Physical and Sensory Disabilities

There are three ways of providing special education for children with physical or sensory impairment: in special residential or day schools for those with specific disabilities; through 'split placement' which includes some mainstream attendance; or within a mainstream school which provides support.

The tendency to regard all physical or sensory impairment as permanently disabling is erroneous. The visually handicapped, provided with text in Braille or audio-equipment, may well cope admirably with integration. The hearing impaired benefit from modern hearing aids, lip reading and speech therapy. Legislation requires that all areas of schools designed since the mid-1970s are accessible to those with orthopaedic conditions affecting mobility. Regrettably funding has not allowed for any but the most elementary modifications to schools built before then.

Pupils with physical or sensory impairment may need support, depending on the extent of that impairment and the age at which remediation began. For some pupils that support may be given by peers within the classroom and the school building, an important aspect of integration. More frequently there is need of a support assistant. Because the class or subject teacher is responsible for the content and direction of the lesson, there is need for sound preparation by and close collaboration between teacher and assistant:

the relative parameters of their roles must be clearly understood. The support assistant is also a valuable further contact with parents, ensuring that the learning processes begun in the school are continued within the home. It is essential that these children receive wherever possible the enhancement of experiential learning through conversation, visits and those activities of which they are capable.

Modern educational technology is rapidly enhancing the learning potential of disabled children. There are four regional Special Education Micro-electronic Centres which research and advise on aids to learning. The Vincent workstation transcribes Braille into print, making the blind pupil's work instantly accessible and facilitating note-taking. There are computer aids developed for the physically impaired: the Headstart workstation has a head control for those without manual dexterity. Closed circuit television monitors can bring chalkboard work within the limits of vision of the partially sighted.

Physical education, part of the formal curriculum of British schools, need not exclude disabled children, many of whom are able to adapt exercises to suit their physical or sensory limitations. Teachers can advise on suitable activities and should encourage participation.

See Special Educational Needs (3) for behavioural problems.

SPECIAL EDUCATIONAL NEEDS
(3) – Emotional and Behavioural Problems

Within this general category come also children with emotional and behavioural difficulties (EBD). Both in the number and severity of cases these pupils have become a growing problem for UK schools. The general concept of EBD is of pupils who show aggressive and anti-social behaviour: bullying, defiance of authority, abusiveness, non-compliance with rules. Yet this concentration on extrovert behaviour tends to obscure the difficulties of the withdrawn, timid or inhibited child.

Statistical data for the UK are of dubious validity. There are significant regional differences associated with areas of social disadvantage; figures as high as 30 per cent of the school population have been cited. Previously boys have shown far more behavioural problems than girls, although this differentiation is now in decline among teenagers. EBD is not necessarily linked with scholastic performance, though frustration at not being able to perform as well as their peers will sometimes lead to social alienation. The physical manifestations of EBD have become increasingly of concern, with arson of school buildings and vandalism of school equipment a major drain on LEA and school financial resources. The age of onset of EBD has also declined. In some areas children enter primary school already out of control.

Problem-solving and social skills training should be an essential part of the school curriculum, enabling all pupils to consider the consequences of their and their peers' actions. Role-play, simulation, video feedback and discussion are valuable features of this training. Behaviour modification involves home and school, enabling a precise diagnosis of the problem to be made and an intervention plan drawn up with clearly defined objectives. All members of staff must know of the plan and keep the class teacher or tutor informed of both positive and negative developments. In less serious cases self-monitoring is useful, where pupils keep a daily record of progress in which teachers comment on work and behaviour and regular discussion sessions reinforce strengths or explore deviant behaviour. In bullying, the No Blame strategy is an interesting innovation: open discussion between bully and victim takes place in the presence of a teacher or counsellor.

There are special day or residential schools for pupils with severe EBD problems. Whether the social malaise of the post-war generations can be remedied by ever-increasing EBD provision is doubtful.

STAFF DEVELOPMENT

While opportunities for personal professional development always existed – for a higher degree, release from school for attendance at LEA courses and lectures, vacation courses in colleges and universities – LEA funding for these steadily declined in the face of more pressing demands on the budget. Furthermore, headteachers had come to recognize that their priorities for staff development were not necessarily being met. A greater control by the school over matching individual with school needs was called for.

With the publication of DES Circular 3/83 a wide range of management and curricular areas of major concern were identified and the release of teachers to attend them funded from government grants. This funding for prescribed areas of development was known by a succession of acronyms including GRIST (Grant-related In-service Training) and GEST (Grants for Educational Support and Training).

In 1986 training for teacher appraisal was included. The importance of this to the evolution of staff development was not immediately recognized, but discussion at the appraisal interview of the training needs of the appraisee led in many large schools to the remit to a senior member of staff of the responsibility for investigating suitable opportunities for development and making recommendations to the headteacher or senior management team about priorities. Since the institution of local financial management (LFM) governors must agree a training budget and may even require the headteacher to justify the priorities for the use of these funds.

The requirement that each school allocates annually a number of teacher education days when the school is closed to pupils has enabled staff corporately to engage in planning and whole-school development. Programmes of school-based management training, curriculum panel meetings, and topic presentations by a member of staff are also likely to be built into the staff meetings calendar of the school. Any danger that a school might become inbred in its staff development can be overcome by interschool subject or topic consortia and, if teachers can be released, by intervisitation with other schools doing innovative work.

Staff appraisal has highlighted a problem that has always existed but has rarely been tackled efficiently: that of the failing teacher. A particular kind of staff development is called for here, including one-to-one support. Newly qualified teachers (NQTs) also need personal support, usually through a mentor, because they will discover staff development needs that their training, however good, had not anticipated.

STAFFING THE SCHOOL
(1) – Teaching Staff

Schools will have both teaching staff and non-teaching or ancillary staff. All are appointed directly by a committee of governors, or indirectly by delegation to the headteacher.

Teaching staff

The staff of the school is led by the headteacher, known in Scotland and in some areas of England as the principal. England and Wales remain committed to the former term when most other English-speaking countries use the latter. This is because, by long tradition, headteachers undertake some teaching commitment, however small, in addition to managerial responsibilities.

The rest of the staff are known as assistant teachers. There will be one or more deputy heads, known in Scotland as deputes. The role of the deputy is not only to deputise for the headteacher when necessary, but also to take on delegated responsibility. In large comprehensive schools with two deputies, each will usually have specifically delegated functions. There was a time when one had responsibility for pastoral care, the other for curriculum management; with the introduction of school-based management this clear-cut distinction is breaking down.

Class teachers are paid on a national nine-point scale or spine, from point 1 or 2 for the newly qualified teacher (NQT), though previous relevant experience may entitle the NQT to a higher starting point. There is then yearly progression up the scale to the maximum. Teachers with significant assigned managerial responsibilities, middle managers, are placed on a higher level of the spine. In a large comprehensive school up to one-third of the staff will be entitled to incentive allowances. A few will be senior teachers, paid at or near the maximum of the spine. These are likely to be members of the senior management team. Headteachers and deputies have their own salary scales, determined by the size of the school and the number of years in post.

Unless teachers have been appointed to temporary or part-time posts, they have security of tenure provided they remain competent and are not guilty of any serious professional misconduct. However, if the school budget under local financial management declines so that teachers must be dismissed, the governors may seek their relocation to another school, offer voluntary redundancy or, if there is no happier solution, require compulsory redundancy. All teachers have a standard contract which includes conditions of service.

See Staffing the School (2) for ancillary staff.

STAFFING THE SCHOOL (2) – Ancillary Staff

Schools are dependent on the quality of their non-teaching or ancillary staff. Large schools will, since the introduction of local financial management, have either a bursar or a senior secretary skilled in financial management. The headteacher controls budget allocations, but an ancillary controls its day-to-day management: balances are struck regularly, staff are kept informed and over-spending avoided.

The number of full-time equivalent (fte) secretarial staff should be determined by needs analysis but more often depends on the total finances available. Opportunities for training and the rapid development of the use of computer technology have greatly increased the efficiency of what is generally called 'the office'.

The use of radio, film, overhead projectors (OHPs), photo-copiers and other teaching aids requires the employment in a large school of a technician to control use and distribution, order software and service the hardware. Laboratory technicians are employed to prepare materials for class experiments and to maintain equipment.

Because the school day is longer than in most European countries, a midday break is necessary. Born of pre-war malnutrition among many children in urban elementary schools, and maintained in wartime as a means of supplementing the diet of all children, the school dinner remains an institution, even though costs have risen and many children now bring their own food. Supervision of the behaviour of children during and after the school meal is the responsibility of School Meals Supervisory Assistants (SMSAs). At primary school level many SMSAs take a proactive role, encouraging good social behaviour and promoting safe play.

Infant schools have, when funds allow, qualified nursery nurses in the Reception class and Y1 to give support to the teacher, largely with non-teaching activities but also with the supervision of learning activities set up by the teacher. General assistants (GAs) have a similar role with, for example, slow learners or pupils with physical disabilities.

Each school is responsible within its budget for cleaning and maintaining the school premises. Responsible to the headteacher for this is the caretaker – in North America the janitor – and a staff of part-time cleaners. In vacation times major repair work may be undertaken. If a school is a community school, the caretaker's role is extensive and calls for high order managerial skills, since the school is in use in the evenings, at weekends and in vacations.

TEACHER APPRAISAL

In England and Wales teacher appraisal is now compulsory. All teachers, including the headteacher, are appraised on a two-year cycle. The main concern of appraisal is with staff development. It is also a two-way process in which shortcomings in school management may surface. The appraiser is usually a line manager, and a ratio of four appraisees to each appraiser is considered the optimum.

A job specification, regularly updated, must be prepared for each teacher consisting of three elements: the job purpose, the key result areas – groupings of activities where results must be achieved to satisfy the job purpose – and the activities which will deliver the key result areas.

Agreeing goals is an essential feature of appraisal and staff development. The appraiser and appraisee agree goals for the two-year period, only some of which will feature in the appraisal interview. These goals must accord with school policy and therefore must meet with the approval of the senior management team.

Classroom observation is part of the appraisal process. Each teacher is twice observed teaching, shortly before the appraisal interview. Often one lesson is chosen by the appraisee and one by the appraiser. They meet before each lesson to enable the appraisee to explain the form and content of the proposed lesson, and after the lesson for a debriefing.

The appraisal interview usually lasts one hour. The appraisee has had the opportunity to prepare a self-appraisal, either for personal use or to share with the appraiser. The interview covers classroom performance, and the extent to which selected goals have been realized. The appraiser writes a report on the interview which is shown to the appraisee, who has the right to add a note of 'dissent'. New or revised goals will be set in the report. The appraisee's further training needs may well be included for consideration by the senior management team. Appraisal reports are internal to the school and the LEA's officers. Governors are informed only that appraisals have been properly held, and that there may be certain general conclusions for their consideration.

Follow-up is essential. Although there may well be informal meetings from time to time, there is also towards the end of the alternate year a formal follow-up interview between appraisee and appraiser to review progress.

Headteacher appraisal is conducted on similar lines, except that there are two appraisers, a peer headteacher and an LEA inspector or adviser.

TEACHER QUALIFICATION

Almost all teachers in the United Kingdom are qualified through holding a degree, or a degree and a postgraduate certificate.

Degree (Bachelor of Education)

The B.Ed. is a four-year Honours degree awarded by a university. The length of the course may be reduced for a mature student who has some other relevant qualification, in social work for example. For a time, the four-year B.Ed. (Hons) ran alongside a three-year B.Ed.; and before the B.Ed. was introduced there was a two-year Certificate of Education. Most certificated teachers have by now either retired or have 'made up' their qualification to degree standard by full- or part-time study.

Degree and Postgraduate Certificate

The alternative route into teaching is to take a university Honours degree course, usually for three years, leading to a B.A. (Bachelor of Arts), a B.Sc. (Bachelor of Science), or any similar first degree qualification. Prospective teachers add to this a further year's qualification, the Postgraduate Certificate in Education (PGCE). A few universities offer a four-year course integrating academic study with a teaching qualification, where the teaching element is spread over several years.

Alternative routes

Two alternative teacher training routes have been introduced for mature applicants with specific qualifications or experience. The articled teacher is a graduate who has experience in industry or commerce and becomes a trained teacher by taking a school-based PGCE in conjunction with an approved teacher training institution. The licensed teacher lacks graduate status and qualifies through a two-year on-the-job induction programme.

Note: in the United Kingdom, once teachers are qualified, there is no restriction on the age level at which they may teach, though in practice most B.Ed. graduates teach in primary schools, and most subject graduates in secondary schools or corporate colleges.

Higher professional degrees

There is a wide range of higher degrees open to teachers aspiring to promotion to senior posts or wishing to improve their skills and knowledge. These are usually taken part-time, though there are full-time courses, and lead to, for example, the M.A.(Ed.) or M.Ed. The Ed.D combines taught modules and a short thesis. The Ph.D., entirely by thesis, requires a major piece of original educational research. There are also certificates in counselling, special educational needs and a number of other specialisms.

UNIVERSITIES

In the immediate post-war period there was a major building programme both to extend the accommodation of existing universities and to found new ones. Almost all degree-awarding institutions now have university status: both the colleges of advanced technology (CATs) that had been founded alongside the new universities, and more recently all polytechnics. Most colleges of higher education are now absorbed into universities, usually into the former polytechnics. There are still some specialized colleges, mainly for the Arts, and one university, that remain independent.

The nominal head of the university is the Chancellor: an honorary appointment, usually of a distinguished academic or an eminent industrialist. The *de facto* head of the university is the Vice-chancellor, often supported, particularly when a university is on several sites, by Pro-vice-chancellors. In Scotland the Vice-chancellor usually carries the title of Principal and Vice-chancellor.

Every university is composed of a number of semi-autonomous schools, faculties or departments. The precise definition of these terms differs from one university to another. Each will have as its senior academic a professor who will be the dean or director, regardless of whether that title is used. There are likely to be other professors, to cover different fields of learning. UK universities do not use the term assistant professor as in North America, and professorships are therefore considered a high academic distinction. Very occasionally an eminent industrialist or educationist from outside the field of universities may be invited to be a visiting professor. The term reader is used for the next in seniority.

The main university teachers are the principal lecturers, senior lecturers and lecturers. Nowadays, appointments are often made on short-term contracts. The workload of lecturers has increased considerably with an expectation of high contact time with students; yet simultaneously there are increasing expectations that they will publish books and research papers, since a department's funding depends in part on its publicly assessed research rating. Student admissions are another cause of anxiety, since the number qualified to enter university grows annually, class sizes increase, while at the same time universities may compete for those with the highest potential.

The policy-making body of the university is the senate, on which serve some by right of their office, some by election by their peers and some as student representatives.

3
ABBREVIATIONS AND ACRONYMS

AAU	Academic Audit Unit
ACACE	Advisory Council for Adult and Continuing Education
ACAS	Advisory, Conciliation and Arbitration Service
ACC	Association of County Councils
ACE	Advisory Centre for Education
ACFHE	Association of Colleges for Further and Higher Education
AFC	Association for Colleges
AFE	Advanced Further Education
AGCAS	Association of Graduate Careers Advisory Services
A-level	Advanced Level Examination (GCE)
AMA	Association of Metropolitan Authorities
AMG	Annual Maintenance Grant
AMMA	Assistant Masters and Mistresses Association (now ATL)
APL	Accreditation of Prior Learning
APT	Association of Polytechnic Teachers
APU	Assessment of Performance Unit
APVIC	Association of Principals in Sixth Form Colleges
ARCS	Action Research on Change in Schools

ARRE	Association of Recruitment and Retention in Education
ARTEN	Anti-Racist Teacher Education Network
ASB	Aggregated School Budget
ASE	Association of Science Education
AS-level	Advanced Supplementary Level Examination (GCE)
AT	Articled Teacher
AT	Attainment Target
ATL	Association of Teachers and Lecturers
ATM	Association of Teachers of Mathematics
AUR	Alternative Use of Resources
AUT	Association of University Teachers
AVA	Audio-Visual Aids
AWPU	Age Weighted Pupil Unit
B.A.	Bachelor of Arts
BC	British Council
BEC	Business Education Council
B.Ed.	Bachelor of Education
BEI	British Education Index
BEMAS	British Educational Management and Administration Society
BERA	British Educational Research Association
BS 5750	British Standard 5750
B.Sc.	Bachelor of Science
BTEC	Business and Technology Education Council
CAL	Computer-Assisted Learning
CALL	Computer-Assisted Language Learning
CASE	Campaign for the Advancement of State Education
CATE	Council for the Accreditation of Teacher Education
CAT	College of Advanced Technology
CATS	Credit Accumulation and Transfer Scheme
CBE	Competence Based Education
CCT	Compulsory Competitive Tendering
CCTV	Closed Circuit Television
CDT	Craft Design and Technology
CEA	Conservative Education Association
CEDC	Community Education Development Centre

CEE	Certificate of Extended Education
CEF	Colleges Employers' Forum
CEO	Chief Education Officer
CERI	Centre for Educational Research and Innovation
Cert.Ed.	Certificate in Education
CFE	College for Further Education
CHE	College of Higher Education
CHEA	Children's Home-based Education Association
CHEI	Committee of Heads of Educational Institutions
CI	Chief Inspector (of Schools)
CILT	Centre for Information on Language Teaching
CIPFA	Chartered Institute of Public Finance and Accountancy
CLEA	Council of Local Education Authorities
CNAA	Council of National Academic Awards
COHSE	Confederation of Health Service Employees
CPS	Centre for Policy Studies
CPVE	Certificate of Pre-Vocational Education
CRE	Commission for Racial Equality
CSE	Certificate of Secondary Education
CSMS	Concepts in Secondary Mathematics and Science
CTA	Critical Thinking Appraisal
CTC	City Technology College
CVCP	Committee of Vice-Chancellors and Principals
DE	Department of Employment
DENI	Department of Education Northern Ireland
DES	Department of Education and Science (now DFEE)
DFE	Department for Education
DFEE	Department for Education and Employment
DIME	Development of Ideas in Mathematics Education
Dip.Ed.	Diploma in Education
Dip.HE	Diploma of Higher Education
EA	Education Association
EAC	Educational Assessment Centre
EBD	Emotional and Behavioural Difficulties
Ed.D.	Doctor of Education
EFL	English as a Foreign Language
EIS	Educational Institute of Scotland
EMU	Evaluation and Monitoring Unit (of SEAC)
ENIRDEM	European Network for Improving Research and Development in Educational Management

EO	Education Officer
EO	Education Otherwise
EO	Equal Opportunities
EOC	Equal Opportunities Commission
EPA	Educational Priority Area
ERA	Education Reform Act
ERASMUS	European Action Scheme for the Mobility of University Students
ERIC	Educational Resources Information Center
ESG	Education Support Grant
ESL	English as a Second Language
ESN	Educationally Subnormal
ESRC	Economic and Social Science Research Council
ESS	Education Support Staff
ETV	Educational Television
EWO	Education Welfare Officer
EWS	Education Welfare Service
FAS	Funding Agency for Schools
FCO	Foreign and Commonwealth Office
FE	Further Education
FEFC	Further Education Funding Council
FEU	Further Education Unit
FHE	Further and Higher Education
FL	Flexible Learning
fte	full-time equivalent
GA	General Assistant
GCE	General Certificate of Education
GCSE	General Certificate of Secondary Education
GEST	Grants for Education Support and Training.
GM	Grant Maintained
GMS	Grant Maintained School
GMSC	Grant Maintained Schools Centre
GNVQ	General National Vocational Qualifications
GRE	Grant-Related Expenditure
GRIDS	Guidelines for Review and Internal Development in Schools
GRIST	Grant Related In-Service Training
GSB	General School Budget
GTC	General Teaching Council
GTTR	Graduate Teacher Training Registry

HE	Higher Education
HEA	Health Education Authority
HEFCE	Higher Education Funding Council for England
HEI	Higher Education Institution
HEIST	Higher Education Information Services Trust
HMC	Headmasters' Conference
HMCI	Her Majesty's Chief Inspector of Schools
HMI	Her Majesty's Inspectorate
HMSO	Her Majesty's Stationery Office
HNC	Higher National Certificate
HND	Higher National Diploma
HoD	Head of Department
HoF	Head of Faculty
HoH	Head of House
HoY	Head of Year
IAPS	Incorporated Association of Preparatory Schools
IB	International Baccalaureate
ICG	Institute of Careers Guidance
ICRA	International Centre for Research on Assessment
IDP	Institutional Development Plan
IHE	Institute of Higher Education
II	Independent Inspector
IIEP	International Institute for Educational Planning
ILEA	Inner London Education Authority
IMA	Institute of Mathematics and its Applications
IMTEC	International Movement Towards Educational Change
INSET	In-Service Education and Training
ISIS	Independent Schools Information Service
IT	Information Technology
ITE	Initial Teacher Education
ITT	Initial Teacher Training
JMB	Joint Matriculation Board
KISS	Keep It Short and Simple
KMP	Kent Mathematics Project
KS	Key Stage
LEA	Local Education Authority
LEATGS	Local Education Authority Training Grants Scheme
LFM	Local Financial Management

LMS	Local Management of Schools
LOA	Level of Attainment
LOP	Lesson Observation Proforma
LPA	Local Priority Area
LTS	Licensed Teacher School
MA	Mathematical Association
MBA	Master of Business Administration
MBO	Management by Objectives
MBWA	Management by Walking Around
MD	Management Development or Managing Director
M.Ed.	Master of Education
MEI	Mathematics in Education and Industry
MIS	Management Information System
MPG	Main Professional Grade (now SNS)
M. Phil.	Master of Philosophy
MSD	Management Self-Development
NA	National Assessment
NAESC	National Association for the Education of Sick Children
NAFE	Non-Advanced Further Education
NAGC	National Association for Gifted Children
NAGM	National Association of Governors and Managers
NAHT	National Association of Head Teachers
NAIEA	National Association of Inspectors and Education Advisers
NALGO	National Association of Local Government Employees
NAPE	National Association for Primary Education
NASSP	National Association of Secondary School Principals
NAS/UWT	National Association of Schoolmasters/Union of Women Teachers
NATE	National Association for the Teaching of English
NATFHE	National Association of Teachers in Further and Higher Education
NAYCEO	National Association of Youth and Community Education Officers
NC	National Curriculum
NCA	National Curriculum Assessment
NCC	National Curriculum Council

NCE	National Commission on Education
NCET	National Council for Educational Technology
NCPTA	National Confederation of Parent–Teacher Associations
NCT	Non-Contact Time
NCVQ	National Council for Vocational Qualifications
NDCEMP	National Development Centre for Educational Management and Policy
NEA	Northern Examining Group
NEC	National Extension College
NEOST	National Employers' Organization for School Teachers
NFER	National Foundation for Education Research
NGC	National Governors' Council
NGO	Non-Governmental Organization
NIACE	National Institute of Adult Continuing Education
NLP	Neuro-linguistic Programming
NQT	Newly Qualified Teacher
NRA	National Record of Achievement
NSG	National Steering Group
NSSE	National Society for the Study of Education
NTS	Non-Teaching Staff
NUPE	National Union of Public Employees
NUT	National Union of Teachers
NVQ	National Vocational Qualification
OD	Organizational Development
OFSTED	Office for Standards in Education
OHMCI	Office of Her Majesty's Chief Inspector
OHP	Overhead Projector
O-level	Ordinary Level Examination (GCE)
ONC	Ordinary National Certificate
OND	Ordinary National Diploma
ORACLE	Observational Research and Classroom Learning Evaluation
OU	Open University
PAL	Peer Assisted Leadership
PAT	Professional Association of Teachers
PC	Parents' Charter
PC	Profile Component (National Curriculum)
PCAS	Polytechnic and Colleges Admissions System (now combined with UCCA)

PCFC	Polytechnic and Colleges Funding Council
PE	Physical Education
PFI	Private Finance Initiative
PGCE	Post Graduate Certificate in Education
Ph.D.	Doctor of Philosophy
PI	Performance Indicator
PICKUP	Professional Industrial and Commercial Updating
PICSI	Pre-inspection Context and School Indicator
PL	Principal Lecturer
PMU	Project Management Unit
POS	Programmes of Study
POSE	Schools' Council Projection on Statistical Education
PPA	Pre-school Playgroups Association
PPQ	Personal Preference Questionnaire
PRB	Pay Review Body
PRP	Performance-Related Pay
PRR	Pupils' Registration Regulations
PSB	Potential Schools Budget
PSE	Personal and Social Education
PSHE	Personal, Social and Health Education
PT	Part-time
PTA	Parent–Teacher Association
PTR	Pupil : Teacher Ratio
QA	Quality Assurance
QAU	Quality Audit Unit
QTS	Qualified Teacher Status
QUANGO	Quasi-autonomous non-Governmental Organization
R and D	Research and Development
RBL	Resource Based Learning
R, D and D	Research, Development and Dissemination
RE	Religious Education
RGI	Registered General Inspector
RLDU	Resources for Learning Development Unit
RSA	Royal Society of Arts
RSG	Revenue Support Grant (formerly Rate Support Grant)
SACRE	The Standing Advisory Committee on Religious Education

SAT	Standard Assessment Task
SATRO	Science and Technology Regional Organization
SCAA	School Curriculum and Assessment Council
SCDC	School Curriculum Development Committee
SCEA	Service Children's Education Authority
SCI	Senior Chief Inspector (HMI)
SCMC	Schools Council Mathematics Committee
SCOTVEC	Scottish Vocational Education Council
SCUE	Standing Conference on University Entrance
SCWG	Schools Council Working Group
SDP	School Development Plan
SEA	Socialist Education Association
SEAC	Schools Examination and Assessment Council
SEC	Secondary Examinations Council
SED	Scottish Education Department
SEG	Southern Examining Group
SEN	Special Educational Needs
SENCO	Special Educational Needs Co-ordinator
SEO	Society of Education Officers
SGTC	Scottish General Teaching Council
SHA	Secondary Heads' Association
SIMS	Schools Information Management System
SL	Senior Lecturer
SLA	School Leaving Age
SLA	School Library Association
SLAPONS	School Leaver Attainment Profile on Numerical Skills
SLS	School Library Service
SMILE	Secondary Mathematics Individualized Learning Experiment
SMP	School Mathematics Project
SMSA	School Meals Supervisory Assistant
SMT	Senior Management Team
SMTF	School Management Task Force
SNA	Special Needs Assistant
SNS	Standard National Scale
SoA	Statement of Attainment
SPIR	The School Performance Information Regulations
SPP	Surplus Pupil Places
SSA	Standard Spending Assessment

SSE	School Self-evaluation
SSR	Staff : Student Ratio
SSS	Supported Self-Study
STA	Socialist Teachers' Association
STOPP	Society of Teachers Opposed to Physical Punishment
STRB	School Teachers' Review Body
SWOT	Strengths, Weaknesses, Opportunities, Threats
TA	Teacher Assessment
TA	Training Agency (Previously MSC)
TANEA	Towards a New Education Act
TASC	Teaching as a Career Unit
TC	Training Commission
TEC	Training and Enterprise Council
TEED	Training Enterprise and Education Directorate (formerly MSC, TC, TA)
TEFL	Teaching English as a Foreign Language
TES	Times Educational Supplement
TGAT	Task Group on Assessment and Training
THES	Times Higher Education Supplement
TIQL	Teacher–Pupil Interaction and Quality of Learning
TPCSB	Teachers' Pay and Conditions of Service Body
TQM	Total Quality Management
TRIST	TVEI-Related In-Service Training
TSS	Testing of Strategic Skills
TTA	Teacher Training Agency
TVE	Technical and Vocational Education
TVEE	Technical and Vocational Education Extension
TVEI	Technical and Vocational Education Initiative
U3A	University of the Third Age
UCAS	Universities and Colleges Admissions Service
UCCA	Universities Central Council on Admissions
UCET	Universities Council for the Education of Teachers
UDE	University Department of Education
UFC	Universities Funding Council
UGC	University Grants Committee
UNISON	The union resulting from the amalgamation of COHSE, NALGO and NUPE

VA	Voluntary Aided
VC	Vice-Chancellor
VC	Voluntary Controlled
VET	Vocational Education and Training
VQ	Vocational Qualifications
VRQ	Verbal Reasoning Quotient
VS	Voluntary Schools
WEA	Workers' Education Association
WEF	World Education Fellowship
YOP	Youth Opportunities Programme
YT	Youth Training
YTS	Youth Training Scheme
ZBB	Zero-base Budgeting

BIBLIOGRAPHY

Gordon, P. and Lawton, D. (1984) *A Guide to English Educational Terms*, Batsford Academic and Educational Ltd, London.

Johannsen, H. and Page, G. T. (1990) *International Dictionary of Management*, Kogan Page, London.

Lawton, D. and Gordon, P. (1993) *Dictionary of Education*, Hodder & Stoughton, Sevenoaks.

McLeish, K. J. (1993) *Guide to Human Thought*, Bloomsbury Publishing Ltd, London.

McLeod, W. T. (1985) *The New Collins Concise Dictionary of the English Language*, Guild Publishing, London.

Pemberton, J. E. (1973) *British Official Publications*, Pergamon Press, Oxford.

Rosenberg, J. M. (1993) *Dictionary of Business and Management*, John Wiley & Sons Inc., New York.

Rowntree, D. (1981) *A Dictionary of Education*, Kogan Page, London.